Student Discipline

Student Discipline

A Prosocial Perspective

Edited by Philip M. Brown

ROWMAN & LITTLEFIELD
Lanham • Boulder • New York • London

Published by Rowman & Littlefield
A wholly owned subsidiary of The Rowman & Littlefield Publishing Group, Inc.
4501 Forbes Boulevard, Suite 200, Lanham, Maryland 20706
www.rowman.com

Unit A, Whitacre Mews, 26-34 Stannary Street, London SE11 4AB

Previous book by Philip M. Brown: *Handbook of Prosocial Education*

British Library Cataloguing in Publication Information Available

Library of Congress Cataloging-in-Publication Data

Names: Brown, Philip M., 1942– editor of compilation.
Title: Student discipline : a prosocial perspective / edited by Philip M. Brown.
Description: Lanham : Rowman & Littlefield, [2016] | Includes bibliographical references and index.
Identifiers: LCCN 2015040844 (print) | LCCN 2015049430 (ebook) | ISBN 9781475813975 (hardback : alk. paper) | ISBN 9781475813982 (pbk.) | ISBN 9781475813999 (electronic)
Subjects: LCSH: School discipline. | Problem children—Behavior modification. Classification: LCC LB3012 .S87 2016 (print) | LCC LB3012 (ebook) | DDC 371.5—dc23
LC record available at http://lccn.loc.gov/2015040844

∞ ™ The paper used in this publication meets the minimum requirements of American National Standard for Information Sciences Permanence of Paper for Printed Library Materials, ANSI/NISO Z39.48-1992.

Printed in the United States of America

Discipline is a teaching-learning kind of relationship as the similarity of the word disciple *suggests. By helping our children learn to be self-disciplined, we are also helping them learn how to become independent of us as, sooner or later, they must. And we are helping them learn how to be loving parents of children of their own.*

—Fred Rogers, *Wisdom from the World According to Mister Rogers*

Contents

Foreword: Prosocial Education for American Democracy

Institutional experiences are vital to political socialization and, at least in the case of children and youth, to developing the skills and dispositions that can promote democracy. Harry Eckstein called this "congruence" in his theory of stable democracy. Alexis De Tocqueville applied a similar logic to civil juries in a book he wrote to describe American democracy in the 1830s. Juries, he argued, "teach men equity in practice. Each man, when judging his neighbor, thinks that he may be judged himself. . . . Juries teach each individual not to shirk responsibility for his own acts . . . they make all men feel that they have duties toward society and that they take a share in its government. By making men pay attention to things other than their own affairs, they combat that individual selfishness which is like rust in society." If jury participation can have such an impact on the individual, schools can have even greater impact on our society, as schools are universal, and experiences in schools affect life outcomes, student's views of other students, and their sense of self, both as a person and in relationship to others.

Although these lessons are true for all students, these experiences convene racial messages that Tocqueville in the 1830s was not prepared to address. Think about the particular messages that African American students receive when they are disproportionately disciplined, segregated from other students by being placed in special classes where the other students are largely or only students of color. And think about the message they and their peers receive when they are removed from school, as some are, in the same type of manacles that were used to contain and discipline Africans and African Americans during slavery. Although these messages are subjective they have objective counterparts: how school discipline contributes to grade retention to both drop out and the school to prison pipeline.

As these examples suggest, school discipline is not just a technical matter or a small matter. In the words of Secretary of Education Arne Duncan "every single year, our K-12 schools suspend roughly three and a half million students, and refer a quarter of million children to the police for arrest. If our collective goal is to end the school to prison pipeline, that is simply unacceptable" (U. S. Department of Education, 2015). The values of democracy, equality, fairness, and inclusiveness are fundamental to the analyses of school discipline. So is our understanding of how students learn to be responsible and active members of schools and communities.

Positive experiences with self-discipline and community- and relationship-based discipline can prepare students to be active, reflective, and compassionate citizens—ones who see themselves and others who are different from them as part of public intuitions and believe that alone and that they can help make these institutions for the better. However, experiences with externally imposed control and harsh and punitive discipline can do the opposite: these negative approaches don't teach self-control and social responsibility. In addition, they contribute to alienation from adults and schools, reactive oppositional behavior (Willis, 1977), and the acceptance of a might-makes-right approach public order and private affairs.

These ideas are not novel nor outside of the American tradition. Thomas Jefferson and Horace Mann, America's first Secretary of Education (in Massachusetts), viewed education as preparing citizens to participate in democratic governance. In fact, Mann, who is often considered the father of the modern public school, attacked corporal punishment, stating that schools should build upon "That powerful class of motives which consists of affection for parents, love for brothers and sisters, whether older or younger than themselves, justice and the social sentiment toward schoolmates, respect for elders, the pleasures of acquiring knowledge, the duty of doing as we would be done by, the connection between present conduct, and success, estimation, eminence, in future life" (Mann, 1844, p. 131). Seventy-two years later a more modern democrat, John Dewey, critiqued external discipline and called for self-discipline that builds upon students' interests.

The school, Dewey suggested, can become "a form of social life, a miniature community" and that student's experience of active participation and learning to self-manage prepared them to be active citizens (Dewey, 1916). This approach can work. Research indicates that constructivist social and emotional learning programs such as Open Circle and The Responsive Classroom can build classroom community while improving student discipline. One example of the kind of evidence-based approaches included in this volume is the Caring School Communities (CSC) program (see chapter 5 for a fuller description), which I have reported on previously. CSC (quoting from a report my colleague Yael Kidron and I wrote for the What Works Clearinghouse) employs class meetings, cross-age "buddies" programs, "homeside" activities, which link family and school, and school-wide community-building activities.

Socially, CSC has been demonstrated to (in comparison to control elementary schools) create a stronger sense of community, stronger commitment to democratic values, greater concern for others, improved conflict-resolution skills, and a stronger commitment to learning. Its effects appear to persist into middle schools and were related to higher grades and test scores, less misconduct and delinquency, a stronger sense of community, and more commitment to higher education.

Although neither novel nor undoable, these positive approaches to self-discipline were and are not dominant. For example, a Boston schoolmaster, Thomas Hale, retorted to Mann in 1844, that "[P]hysical coercion is, in certain cases, necessary, natural, and proper." Or, to use another example, the First Annual Report of the U.S. Commissioner of Education (1886) reported on "An Experiment in Discipline" where a San Francisco principal used one of his teachers to create a segregated class for behaviorally challenging students. These punitive approaches to school discipline have persisted until today. In fact the use of harsh, punitive, and exclusionary discipline increased between 1990 and 2010, as did racial disparities in the impact of exclusionary discipline.

Like the 1886 California principal, some educators and policymakers argue that exclusionary and punitive approaches are necessary because of oppositional students and their families. Others don't blame students but justify negative approaches by talking about the needs of students or their families. Although the needs exist, the use of these needs to justify the use of exclusionary discipline is not supported by research that controls for student demographics. In fact, an increasing body of research suggests that cultural, structural, policy, pedagogical, and student support factors that are created by educators—not demographic factors—provide a better explanation. For example, state-wide studies in Texas and Virginia determined that schools with similar demographics produce very different results (Cornell, 1998; Council of State Governments, 2011) and studies that looked across many states suggest that educators can proactively prevent "zero tolerance behaviors," and that this can happen in racially diverse settings. (Quinn et al., 1998; Sandler, 2000; Osher, Sandler, & Nelson, 2001).

Reactive, punitive, and exclusionary approaches to discipline lack empirical support. Research demonstrates that punishment does not help students learn to discipline themselves and that zero tolerance does not work. Experimental and longitudinal analyses demonstrate that harsh approaches to preventing delinquency (e.g., Scared Straight, Boot Camps, incarceration, segregating, and cluster "anti-social" students) are ineffective and, that, in fact, they often have iatrogenic effects and produce a negative return on investment.

So why do harsh and exclusionary approaches persist? The issue is in part epistemological and ideological. Discipline is often equated with external discipline and punishment, as is pointed out in the first chapter of this volume. Approaches such as zero tolerance are (in the words of two Canadian scholars) part "of the episteme of standardized solutions to complex problems" (Daniel & Bondy, 2008) as well as taken-for-grantedness that punishment works. In the United States this even includes a U.S. Supreme Court Decision (Ingraham v. Wright, 430 U.S. 651 [1977]), in which the justices refused to view paddling that resulted in hematomas as cruel and unusual punishment.

The belief that exclusionary discipline is normal is not the case in countries such as Finland where suspension is not part of the policy repertoire and viewed as making no sense in a country committed to universal compulsory education. When educators use student demographics as an explanation for discipline measures that have the effect of excluding students, they are employing what William Ryan described as victim-blaming approaches (Ryan, 1972). Such approaches only look at the student or family, not at ecological factors and solutions that attempt to change the student, without addressing the elements of the school environment that contribute to disorder and indiscipline. Although one can employ victim-blaming approaches without being prejudiced, implicit biases, which are reinforced by stereotype priming and segregated experiences, can exacerbate the impact of victim-blaming approaches and contribute to what sociologists call aversive racism.

Policy and resource allocation are also important here. The individualist victim-blaming approaches are reinforced by policies that focus on individual and school test performance and do not emphasize the importance of ensuring that there are opportunities to learn and conditions for learning that that can work for all students. Finland, to use the same national counterfactual, not only provides for free public heath but also that schools have behavioral support teams for students and that students and teachers have mandated fifteen-minute break times between classes—to crash, refocus, distress, get a cup of coffee, play, or use the lavatory. The Finnish example is not irrelevant. Although Finland is small, it is larger than some American states, and although it appears ethnically homogenous these policies also exist in East Helsinki schools that serve culturally and linguistically diverse immigrant communities.

Fortunately, these exclusionary approaches are now being challenged by federal, state, local, and foundation efforts that call for improving conditions for learning, reducing exclusionary discipline, employing supportive discipline practices, eliminating discipline disparities, and employing the approaches of positive youth development. Vetted Federal materials describing these approaches and programs are available at the National Center on Safe and Supportive Learning and Environments and Youth.gov. Other materials can be found on the National Clearing House on Supportive School Discipline.

The chapters in this book add to our understanding of how educators can support prosocial learning in a manner that supports student social, emotional, and ethical development. If educators adopt such approaches and succeed with them they will contribute to building a democratic society, which is quite different from those that Thomas Jefferson and Horace Mann envisioned—but an inclusive democratic society that provides equal voice to girls and boys, young women and young men children and youth of color, students who are LBGTQ, and others who have been historically disenfranchised or asked to live in what Paulo Freire called "a culture of silence."

—David Osher
Vice President and Institute Fellow
American Institutes for Research

Preface

The current picture of student discipline in the United States is a mélange of conventional ideas about maintaining rules and order in the classroom (managing student behavior), failed policies such as zero tolerance that emanated from the justifiable fear of children on illicit drugs, and the persuasive impact of behavior management techniques on school strategies. It is widely acknowledged now that school discipline systems play a significant role in the school to prison pipeline (U.S. Department of Education, 2014; Ravitch, 2010).

Equally important to a contemporary understanding of student discipline and school administration of discipline is the growing influence of the different threads of prosocial education (Brown, Corrigan, and D'Alessandro, 2012). Prosocial education anchors the educational enterprise in the science of developmental psychology and related theories and practices of character and moral education, school climate improvement, and social-emotional learning (Berkowitz, 2012; Bear, 2010).

Discipline must go beyond compliance with rules if we are to take the goal of whole-child development seriously. It's true that the causes of some student misbehavior are rooted in the inequities of our social fabric—economic and social conditions that foster inadequate early childhood development, for example. However, school structures and adult relationships also matter a great deal in determining how discipline affects student engagement with social norms.

I am reminded of the first high school principal I consulted with as a young social scientist supported by juvenile justice and delinquency prevention funding in a working-class Pittsburgh suburb in the 1970s. He was uneasy about some of the humanistic ideas I was discussing with his teachers, and let me know that he was happy "when the kids are like cows chewing their cud." No troubles, no problems, and no learning, I thought to my-self.

Most educators would agree that developing self-discipline is critical to the essential American democratic values of individual rights and self-governance. As Larri Nucci (2009) points out so articulately, our moral and ethical obligations as educators ask us to do more than develop young people who are caring and fair; we need them to be able to balance self-interest with justice and compassion. In his view the challenge is no less than "developing individuals capable of lifelong moral growth and who are motivated to con-tribute to the morality of social institutions and the general society" (3–4). To do less, he argues, would be to condemn us to repeating the same mistakes as our forbearers.

Our national infatuation with the idea that we can solve our social ills by getting tough on crime began with Richard Nixon. It ramped up considerably with the war on drugs that legitimately frightened the general public, which then called on schools to play their part in saving young people's lives. In the process, Congress, the courts, and legislators at all levels got in on the act.

Now it's time for a major course correction. The U.S. Departments of Justice and Education have gotten on board, noting the disproportionate rep-resentation of minorities who are shunted to the juvenile justice system. But the truth is that none of us are served when discipline itself is understood only as rules and laws, not as a life-long developmental process. The purpose of this book is to make a small contribution to that course correction.

Acknowledgments

I am grateful to the many colleagues and school staff who have contributed to bringing this book to fruition. Tom Koerner, vice president and publisher of the Education Division of Rowman & Littlefield supported the vision of the book from the beginning. Veronica Moul and Jennifer Littel contributed editing assistance. With the exception of chapters 1 and 2, the chapters or sections were authored by colleagues or coauthored, as noted. In other cases it was a collaborative effort, and those contributing are indicated below:

Chapter 3: Systemic Approaches

The Achieving with Integrity Project
   Authors: David B. Wangaard, president, the School for Ethical Education and Jason M. Stephens, senior lecturer, Faculty of Education and Social Work, the University of Auckland.
Restorative Practices
   Coauthor: John Bailie, president, the International Institute for Restorative Justice.
   Lindsey Miller, intern, the National School Climate Center.
   Anne Gregory, associate professor, Graduate School of Applied and Professional Psychology, Rutgers University.
The Virginia Student Threat Assessment Program
   Kisha Laurent, intern, National School Climate Center.
Positive Behavior Interventions and Supports
   Author: Sharon Lohrmann, director, New Jersey Positive Behavior Support in Schools, the Boggs Center, and assistant professor of Pediatrics, Rutgers Robert Wood Johnson Medical School Department of Pediatrics.

Chapter 4: Curriculum and Instructional Approaches

The Second Step Program
   Coauthors: Bridgid Norman, program development manager, and Tia Kim, director of programs, partnerships, and research, Committee for Children.
The Learning to Breathe Program
   Patricia Broderick, research associate, Prevention Research Center, the Pennsylvania State University.

Chapter 5: Programmatic Approaches

The Community Caring School Program
   Coauthor: Peter Brunn, vice president for organizational learning and communications, Center for the Collaborative Classroom.
The Playworks Program
   Author: Jill Vialet, founder and CEO, Playworks.
The Responsive Classroom Program
   Author: Mary Beth Forton, director of publications and community, the Northeast Foundation for Children.
The Ripple Effects Program
   Author: Alice Ray, cofounder and CEO, Ripple Effects.

Chapter 6: Targeted Approaches

The Peer Group Connection Program
   Author: Sherry Barr, vice president of operations, product management, and evaluation, the Center for Supportive Schools.
Alternative Education Programs
   Author: Robert Eichorn, president, the National Alternative Education Association; and principal, New Directions Alternative School.

Chapter 7: School Profiles

Leataata Floyd Elementary School
   Coauthor: Billy Aydlett, former principal, Leataata Floyd Elementary School.
Marcus Garvey Elementary School
   Coauthors: Michelle Van Allen, principal and staff, Marcus Garvey Elementary School, and Juliet Kandel, U.S. partnerships manager, Committee for Children.
Stewartsville Elementary School
   Coauthor: Susan Mele, principal, Stewartsville Elementary School.
Charles Boehm Middle School

Coauthor: Theresa Ricci, principal, Charles Boehm Middle School.

Cherry Hill Alternative High School

Authors: James Riordan, principal, and Neil Burti, former principal, Cherry Hill Alternative High School.

Lake Braddock Secondary School

Authors: Amy M. Soos, assessment coach, and David Thomas, principal and team, Lake Braddock Secondary School.

Scarsdale Alternative School

Author: Howard Rodstein, director, Scarsdale Alternative School.

Jerome Harrison Elementary School

Coauthor: Carter Welch, principal, Jerome Harrison Elementary School.

Chapter 8: The U.S. Department of Education's Discipline Guidelines

The U.S. Department of Education's Guiding Principles on School Discipline

Author: Jessica Savage, policy and legal director, National School Climate Center.

The Impact of the U.S. Department of Education Discipline Guidelines

Author: David Nash, director of legal education, the Foundation for Educational Administration (the professional development arm of the New Jersey Principal and Supervisor's Association).

Introduction

This book is an attempt to grapple with the fundamental tension between running a public institution responsible for youth development in an orderly fashion that is conducive to learning, and the need to utilize the best science and knowledge based on experience to focus unremittingly on children's growth, not just compliance to imposed rules. As Bryk, Bomez, Grunow, and LeMahier (2014) has recently pointed out, we all learn best when we try our hardest and learn from our mistakes in collaboration with our peers. We have a lot to learn from each other when it comes to school discipline.

This volume does not attempt to offer one key strategy that should address everyday classroom discipline issues; there are many "how to" books offering such advice. Chapter 1 presents my view of some of the important issues and evidence that may help guide the reader to a better way of thinking through these tensions; it contextualizes a more robust sense of discipline than our traditions have offered.

Chapter 2 provides a unique view and structure regarding codes of student conduct, the critical procedural manual for almost all school district discipline policies. Three New Jersey school districts agreed to participate in a two-year pilot project devoted to a complete revision of their student codes of conduct between 2006 and 2008, sponsored in part by a Character Education Program grant from the U.S. Department of Education. The Cherry Hill, Highland Park, and Montvale district administrators, staff, and communities stayed committed throughout the process. The results of their efforts are presented as a foundation for a prosocial approach to school rules.

The programs and approaches in chapters 3–6 were chosen to highlight both mainstream programmatic strategies as well as unique examples of approaches that show strong evidence for success, or cover ground that receives inadequate attention. Many of my colleagues have issues with the

Positive Behavior Intervention and Supports (PBIS) program supported with significant funding from the U.S. Department of Education, because it relies on a behavior contingency approach that research does not show builds intrinsic values and moral reasoning. While I share many of their reservations, PBIS deserves and has a strong representation because it has become such a prevalent policy and program choice of many state agencies and local school districts.

Chapters 3–6 also include content that emphasizes areas related to student life and moral development, such as the importance of play, stress reduction, and academic integrity that do not receive adequate attention when educators think about discipline. Some of the program descriptions provide information on approaches that are consistent with developmental science, such as Second Step and Ripple Effects, or offer alternatives to traditional disciplinary practices, such as restorative justice and the Peer Group Connection. The reader is invited to see the Web sites of the programs included here or contact them directly and see if there may be a match between your needs and the kind of assistance they are capable of offering.

Chapter 7 profiles stories written by educators who have faced real odds and were devoted to continuous improvement of their school climate, including, but not limited to, discipline. The schools included were identified by a range of sources, mainly organizations with a long track record of successfully supporting school change. One of the common threads behind all of their stories is that no one program or strategy is sufficient to make lasting change in student academic success and social growth. Schools are complex institutions with a challenging mission, not warehouses for test-takers.

In order to keep the size of the book more manageable, only a brief introduction to each school's story is included here. Follow the link to the full school profiles on the School Climate Resource Center of the National School Climate Center Web site. I am grateful to Jonathan Cohen for agreeing to host the school stories on his center's site.

Because of the unprecedented attention the U.S. Departments of Education and Justice have placed on reducing the disproportionate disciplinary sanctions levied against minority students, the final chapter outlines both the recommendations that have emerged from that work, as well as some important caveats that educators need to take seriously if they are to play a constructive role, not only in avoiding sanctions themselves, and helping to ameliorate the problem, but in contributing to long-term solutions.

Chapter One

School Discipline

A Prosocial Perspective

Philip M. Brown

School discipline policies have been under considerable scrutiny in recent years. Policymakers, research scientists, and educators alike have shared growing concerns over the negative effects of zero-tolerance policies that have aimed to set a high bar for student misconduct and the inflexible disciplinary practices that have become the norm for many school systems (American Psychological Association Zero Tolerance Task Force, 2008).

The evidence has gradually grown that these strictly enforced, rule-bound frameworks and practices have negatively affected the educational prospects of many students, particularly those of color (Mayer, 1995; Fabelo, Thompson, Plotkin, Carmichael, Marchbanks, and Booth, 2011; Balfanz, Byrnes, and Fox, 2012; Morgan, Salomon, Plotkin, and Cohen, 2014).

In response to this equity issue, on January 2014, the U.S. Department of Education released a package of resources on school discipline for the purpose of providing guidance designed to help correct discriminatory school discipline practices and address the needs of students with behavior problems. (See chapter 8 for a summary of this guidance and the legal implications.)

The underlying issues surrounding school discipline are complex, and go beyond any single perspective or measure. There are societal issues that bear on the behavior and misbehavior of children in school, such as poverty, child-rearing practices, and whether children believe they have a positive role to play in their community and a future in the country's economy.

There are also educational governance and human relations issues that can negatively impact the disciplinary environment, such as a lack of social trust among the adults in a school or an authoritarian leadership structure with no opportunities for student or teacher participation in problem solving. Whether the culture and climate of schools fosters a prosocial or antisocial behavioral environment is largely dependent on whether these issues are handled with intelligence and care, or are neglected out of ignorance or mismanagement.

DISCIPLINE: CONTROL AND PUNISHMENT OR MORALITY AND GROWTH?

Most experienced teachers and school administrators know that the meaning and impact of misconduct is mediated by the specific context in which an event occurs and by the individual characteristics of the offender. The same behavior, such as bringing a knife to school, exhibited by different children or children of different ages does not mean the same thing. And of course context also matters just as much: Was the knife provided by mom in the lunch kit of the seven-year-old, or was it a switch-blade brought in by a fifteen-year-old gang member? So, rules are frequently bent in order to achieve a desired conclusion or remedy a situation that could become worse if not handled adroitly.

For example, a new principal is confronted by an angry mother whose nine-year-old child's new shirt had been torn in an altercation with another boy. The parent is seeking retribution and wants to know how the other boy will be punished. The principal realizes a few minutes into the exchange that a significant part of the parent's anger is due to her inability to buy a new shirt because of the level of poverty the family lives with. He is confronted with the essential question: Is the important thing to determine who was at fault in the incident and apply the appropriate school rule, or to involve both boys in determining how the shirt will be replaced? Different discipline systems and school administrators would answer this question differently.

Most discipline matters involve this dynamic of interpreting behaviors in the context of desired outcomes. It is important to explore this broad landscape in the context of history, which has informed generations of American educators regarding their responsibilities in handling school discipline. First things first: Discipline is defined by two eminent sources as:

- Control that is gained by requiring that rules or orders be obeyed and punishing bad behavior; a way of behaving that shows a willingness to obey rules or orders; behavior that is judged by how well it follows a set of rules or orders; control gained by enforcing obedience or order; a rule or

system of rules governing conduct or activity; training that corrects, molds, or perfects the mental faculties or moral character; and self-control (discipline, Merriam-Webster, n.d).
- The practice of training people to obey rules or a code of behavior, using punishment to correct disobedience (discipline, Oxford Dictionaries, n.d.).

It's interesting to note that both sources indicate that the derivation of the word comes from the Anglo-French and Latin *disciplina*, which means "teaching" and from *discipulus*, or "pupil." The very nature of how we think about discipline is intimately bound to teacher-student relationship.

Whether it is a district code of conduct, classroom rules, or a verbal reprimand, discipline is about how relationships are conducted and managed for an articulated or assumed purpose. There are, then, three themes that constantly interplay when we look at what discipline means and how we are to understand its uses in schools:

1. A set of rules regarding behavior and conduct;
2. The control of student behavior in conformance to these rules; and
3. The training of students in the skills to perfect their moral character and self-control.

Only the third of these three definitions has a basis in values and morality. The lesson here is important: Discipline may be either guided by a moral purpose or framework or be essentially amoral. The Gestapo was a highly disciplined military force with rigorous standards for conduct, and individuals and groups as diverse as Olympic athletes, a jazz quartet, a ballet star, and physicians who work for Doctors Without Borders are all highly disciplined. They all share performance related values such as persistence and creativity, but not necessarily in the service of a moral purpose.

Schools, on the other hand, do have a primary moral purpose: Providing the setting, guidance, and knowledge necessary to help children develop for the good of society. This role that schools play needs to be crafted thoughtfully, based on our growing understanding of human development as well as the core ethical values that represent our social structure. When we do not carefully examine the assumptions and purpose of our disciplinary theory and practices, the outcomes may not be what we want or expect.

Traditional American education has spent much more time and resources, and mental energy in creating rules, controlling student behavior, and maintaining order than in educating children in the abilities and dispositions that will make them more likely to conform to expectations and mature into effective moral agents and ethical citizens. In doing so, it has ignored lessons from our biological ancestors and recent developmental neuroscience.

Since the 1800s two approaches to school discipline and classroom management have defined how educators have created social space to teach academics and ethical behavior in the confines of school walls. The first uses teacher-centered strategies and rules reinforced by either positive or punitive measures to assure conformance. The second focuses on developing self-discipline within students using both student-centered pedagogy and diverse experiential strategies to engender self-control, self-regulation, and character building that centers more on autonomy and social responsibility than on conformity (Bear, 2010).

PROSOCIAL BEHAVIOR AND OUR PRIMATE ANCESTORS

To educate a man in mind and not in morals is to educate a menace to society.
—Theodore Roosevelt

When we naturally assume that discipline is good for its own sake, we are making the assumption that conformity to a set of rules is good for the one and good for the many; that by behaving appropriately we are doing so for the greater good of our family, community, and society. As social animals some rules enforced by some kind of authority are necessary for survival. Evolutionary biology offers compelling evidence of the instinctual basis for prosocial behaviors. Primate research demonstrates that key lessons from our nearest ancestors about the importance of sharing scarce resources for the well-being of our tribe, have likely been embedded in our genetic makeup (De Waal, 2006).

Fairness

A sense of fairness in primates may be rooted in the nature of dominance in their group's hierarchy. It is a given that dominant primates will receive a bigger piece of the pie than subordinate primates. The dominant members of the group receive more resources, like food and breeding mates, compared to the subordinate members. But because the group is so important to everyone's survival, dominant members of a gorilla group make sure that more vulnerable members, such as a nursing mother, receive a share of the food as well.

Membership in this primate group is bountiful for all members (both dominant and subordinate), and the cost of leaving the group is rather high, so membership itself is a desirable resource (De Waal, 2006). This lesson from our ancestors is at the root of our need for belonging; the sense that membership in our profession, union, school, classroom, club, or gang is important to our sense of well-being and meaning in our lives.

Gratitude

Gratitude as well may have deep evolutionary roots and can help us to understand why we are programmed to work together to create a prosocial culture. The bonding and reciprocity promoted by gratitude are the kinds of behaviors that evolutionary biologists see as essential to the survival of social, mammalian species like us. Frans De Waal of Emory University has found, for example, that chimpanzees remember the individuals who have previously groomed them and return the favor at a later time by sharing food with them (Marsh and Keltner, 2015).

De Waal sees this reciprocal altruism as an elementary form of primate gratitude. It is to the primates' advantage to maintain good, cooperative, working relationships with the others that they rely on, and to learn to act in pleasant, kind, and supportive ways. Particularly for primates with little history and a very new dyadic relationship, reciprocity serves an important function. Doing a favor or meeting the request of another can pay off in the future when they have a favor to request. For the primate group, reciprocity and cooperation ensures that everyone is cared for (De Waal, 2003).

Caring

These prosocial exchanges are learned behaviors for which we humans are genetically predisposed. We recognize our basic urge to care for one another and feel empathy toward another person. We feel drawn to people who willingly offer to help and support others, as we feel called upon to react to situations where we are called upon to help. Any good, early childhood teacher knows how to elicit and encourage these caring responses.

Nel Noddings (2002) locates the roots of social justice and therefore the parameters of our discipline system, our sense of right and wrong behavior, in caring. As she points out, when a caring relationship is not present in schools, "the fault often lies in the structure of classes, rules and evaluations" (Noddings, 2008, 163).

For children to care about their place in the school community, they must have had the experience of being cared for and cared about. If a child's early development is in a loving home, transferring the attachment from parent to teacher is not such a difficult task. If not, it is necessary for the teacher to establish that attachment by providing experiences for the child so that he or she knows what it feels like, and means, to be cared for.

NEUROSCIENCE AND THE MORAL IMPULSE

Recently, neuroscience has had success in locating the precise areas of the brain that relate to empathy and fairness. While the brain finds self-serving behavior emotionally unpleasant, it also finds genuine fairness emotionally uplifting. In other words, the brain works differently when prosocial behavior is exhibited or perceived. The response to situations perceived as fair or unfair is so rapid that the reaction overrules the more deliberate rational mind (Tabibnia, Satpute, and Lieberman, 2008). As three researchers at the University of California Los Angelos put it, faced with a conflict, the brain's default position is to demand a fair deal, thus relying upon one's ability to process empathy and fairness (Association for Psychological Science, 2008).

Adults have an ethical obligation to provide environments that foster full development and the potential for a fulfilling and meaningful life, not just an economically productive one. Brown, Corrigan, and D'Alessandro (2012) use *prosocial education* as an umbrella term that encompasses the philosophy and programs that guide society's goal to foster positive youth development.

A biological metaphor, that of a helix, is an apt visual tool to describe the interrelationship of the strands that comprise prosocial education (see figure 1.1). Consider prosocial education as a helix with strands that include prosocial behavior constructs, the principles of social-emotional, moral, and civic education, as well as academic learning.The constructs of empathy and fairness each have become sources of explanation in building theories supportive of prosocial behavior. In our visual model, these serve as core activating strands for the development of other behaviors and skills. There is currently a considerable amount of neuroscience as well as cognitive and developmental psychology research under way that seeks to learn more about the biological and developmental underpinnings of prosocial attitudes and behavior.

It is important to understand that prosocial education is not just about encouraging educators to implement programs and strategies that contribute to building prosocial behavior conducive to learning, socialization, and development. Prosocial education also asks us to consider how this emerging knowledge helps us better understand how humans think, learn, and act in a social context.

For example, what have we learned from neuroscience about empathy that makes it such a critical concept for understanding the importance of prosocial behavior and prosocial education? First, empathy has been demonstrated to occur in the first years of life, implying that it may have a genetic basis (Zahn-Waxler, Robinson, and Emde, 1992).

Second, both neuroscience research on the mirror neuron system in the brain and developmental theorists commonly ascribe empathy as the mechanism behind understanding self–other differentiation (Jeannerod and Anquetil, 2008). It explains the exhibition of caring behaviors in response to signs of distress or need in others (Hoffman, 2001).

Third, empathy involves both perception and cognition of the emotional states of others, and genetics has been shown to account for the systematic

Prosocial Development

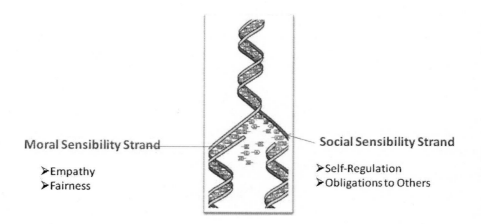

Moral Sensibility Strand

➤Empathy
➤Fairness

Social Sensibility Strand

➤Self-Regulation
➤Obligations to Others

Figure 1.1. A biological metaphor—the genetic basis of prosocial development.

change and relative continuity of empathy over time (Knafo, Zahn-Waxler, Hulle, Robinson, and Rhee, 2008).

As with many human skills, the genetic basis of empathy is important to be aware of because it offers a basis for understanding what we have in common and can take advantage of in fostering personal growth, cohesion, and cooperation. There are two different aspects of empathy: the ability to see the world from the perspective of another; and the ability to imagine what another person is feeling and care about their pain or suffering.

While the empathic tendency may not be evenly distributed among all of us, both aspects of empathy can be learned. It may take some children longer than others, however. Children on the autism spectrum, for example, may have problems reading the cues signaling distress, or have trouble imagining themselves in someone else's shoes, but be very sensitive to others' pain (Szalavitz, 2013). Armed with this knowledge and the kind of approaches and programs represented in this volume, educators have far better methods for developing children's moral sense and social connectedness than implementing zero-tolerance policies for misbehavior.

One contribution that neurobiology can make to school discipline is helping educators better understand the role that early caregiving and stressful conditions both at home and in school play in a student's behavior. If secure attachment to a caregiver is not achieved when children are very young their response to perceived or real threats is compromised (Narvaez, 2014). It is more difficult for them to restore a sense of calm and to develop a repertoire of adaptive responses such as realizing that something that might be scary, like a loud noise, is usually not a threat, or that a cut finger can be cared for and the pain will be temporary.

For a child with insecure attachment to caregivers, a habitual mode of impaired functioning—one that focuses on self-protection—may result. Insecure relationships with caregivers can lead to impaired socioemotional processing as well, which can affect the capacity to learn, to interpret the behavior of others, and to modulate and control basic feelings such as excitement, rage, panic, and hopelessness (Narvaez, 2014; Schore, 2003).

Likewise, stressful conditions can also impede learning to respond and adapt to one's social environment. Children who grow up in high stress homes or neighborhoods may have deficiencies in the natural human ability to feel empathy. They may overreact to situations that are not dangerous, or ignore real danger.

With an unbalanced stress response, a child will find it more difficult to self-regulate and more easily slip into out-of-control mode. When these conditions are a dominant experience, "it's hard to feel compassion or behave in a prosocial manner" (Narvaez, 2014, 143). The good news is that early intervention in combination with skill-based training and a supportive social climate can help to rewire the empathy system and help most children recover their prosocial orientation and behaviors.

SELF-REGULATION

The single most important ability that we learn as we grow up that impacts student and school discipline is self-regulation. Self-regulation involves multiple areas of neuro-anatomy, which refers to different, interrelated parts of the heart-brain system that govern emotion, cognition, and behavior (McCraty, Atkinson, Tomasino, and Bradley, 2006).

The social aspects of functioning are learned as the brain and experience develop together. Self-regulation is a construct that describes how we learn to manage both our thoughts and feelings to enable us to achieve our goals. In order to accomplish this we need to learn to control our impulses and be able to organize and direct our behavior as we face immediate challenges and long-range problems.

The connection between self-regulation and discipline is easy to see. Social competence and positive, prosocial behavior are rooted in a child's growing ability to self-regulate attention, emotion, and behavior. Self-regulation involves the ability to inhibit the expression of behavior and emotion and focus attention. It facilitates the ability to express emotion in constructive ways (Derryberry and Rothbart, 1997; Eisenberg and Fabes, 1992; Murray and Kochanska, 2002).

This connection is important enough that the Administration for Children and Families of the U.S. Department of Health and Human Services has begun a research project (Murray, Rosanbalm, Christopoulos, and Hamoudi, 2015) examining the relationship between self-regulation and toxic stress, the kind of stress that is linked to poverty, inadequate early childhood development, and children living under stressful family conditions. Below are seven key principles from the first report of this work that summarize our current understanding of self-regulation development in context:

1. *Self-regulation serves as the foundation for lifelong functioning* across a wide range of domains, from mental health and emotional well-being to academic achievement, physical health, and socioeconomic success. It has also proven responsive to intervention, making it a powerful target for change.

2. *Self-regulation is defined from an applied perspective as the act of managing cognition and emotion* to enable goal-directed actions such as organizing behavior, controlling impulses, and solving problems constructively.

3. *Self-regulation enactment is influenced by a combination of individual and external factors* including biology, skills, motivation, caregiver support, and environmental context. These factors interact with one another to support self-regulation and create opportunity for intervention.

4. *Self-regulation can be strengthened and taught like literacy*, with focused attention, support, and practice opportunities provided across contexts. Skills that are not developed early on can be acquired later, with multiple opportunities for intervention.

5. *Development of self-regulation is dependent on "co-regulation" provided by parents or other caregiving adults* through warm and responsive interactions in which support, coaching, and modeling are provided to facilitate a child's ability to understand, express, and modulate their thoughts, feelings, and behavior.

6. *Self-regulation can be disrupted by prolonged or pronounced stress and adversity including poverty and trauma experiences.* Although manageable stress may build coping skills, stress that overwhelms children's skills or support can create toxic effects that negatively impact development and produce long-term changes in neurobiology.

7. *Self-regulation develops over an extended period from birth through young adulthood* (and beyond). There are two clear developmental periods where self-regulation skills increase dramatically due to underlying neurobiological changes—early childhood and adoles-

cence—suggesting particular opportunities for intervention. (Murray et al., 2015, 3)

Much of what we know about how to teach self-regulation and create learning environments conducive to learning self-regulation has emerged over the past twenty years as social-emotional learning and school climate improvement research and programs have matured.

SOCIAL-EMOTIONAL LEARNING

Social-emotional learning (SEL) is one of the co-determinants of disciplined, moral behavior, along with individual neruobiology, cultural norms, and social climate. An individual's moral sense emerges from early experience with caregiving and contributes to long-term well-being. But, as Darcia Narvaez puts it so well,

> on a moment-to-moment basis, an individual's morality is a shifting landscape. We move in and out of different ethics based on the social context, our mood, filters, stress response, ideals, goals of the moment, and so on. . . . The trick for most wise behavior is to maintain emotional presence-in-the-moment. Our capacity to spend more time in a prosocial-egalitarian mindset is reliant on well-functioning emotion systems. (Narvaez, 2014, xxvii–xxviii)

What Is Social and Emotional Learning?

Social and emotional learning is the process of acquiring the competencies to recognize and manage emotions, develop caring and concern for others, establish positive relationships, make responsible decisions, and handle challenging situations effectively (Osher et al., 2008; Weissberg, Payton, O'Brien, and Munro, 2007). That is, SEL teaches the personal and interpersonal skills we all need to handle ourselves, our relationships, and our work effectively and ethically. Accordingly, SEL (see table 1.1) is aimed at helping children and even adults develop fundamental skills for success in school and life.

SEL builds from the assumption that educational interventions can be designed to foster children's social and emotional strengths and resiliency. It has been informed by work in child development, classroom management, and public health prevention, as well as the growing understanding of the role of the brain in self-awareness, empathy, and social-cognitive growth (e.g., Best and Miller, 2010; Carter, Harris, and Porges, 2009; Goleman, 2006; Greenberg, 2006). SEL focuses on the skills that allow children to calm themselves when angry, make friends, resolve conflicts respectfully, and make ethical and safe choices (Schonert-Reichl and O'Brien, 2012). SEL offers educators, families, and communities relevant strategies and practices to better prepare students for "the tests of life, not a life of tests" (Elias, 2001).

SEL is grounded in research findings that social and emotional skills can be taught, that they promote developmental assets and reduce problem behaviors, and that they improve children's academic performance, citizenship, and health-related behaviors (e.g., Durlak, Weissberg, Dymnicki, Taylor, and Schellinger, 2011). SEL has been used both as an organizing framework and infused in commercial programs in a wide variety of efforts to prevent drug and alcohol use, reduce conflict, and combat bullying as well as in positive youth development (Devaney, O'Brien, Resnik, Keister, and Weissberg, 2006; Elias et al., 1997).

Table 1.1.　Dimensions of social and emotional learning and related skills.

SEL Dimension	Description
Self-awareness	Accurately assessing one's feelings, interests, values, and strengths; maintaining a well-grounded sense of self-confidence.
Social awareness	Being able to take the perspective of and empathize with others; recognizing and appreciating individual and group similarities and differences; recognizing and using family, school, and community resources.
Self-management	Regulating one's emotions to handle stress, control impulses, and persevere in overcoming obstacles; setting and monitoring progress toward personal and academic goals; expressing emotions appropriately.
Relationship skills	Establishing and maintaining healthy and rewarding relationships based on cooperation; resisting inappropriate social pressure; preventing, managing, and resolving interpersonal conflict; seeking help when needed.
Responsible decision making	Making decisions based on consideration of ethical standards, safety concerns, appropriate social norms, respect for others, and likely consequences of various actions; applying decision-making skills to academic and social situations; contributing to the well-being of one's school and community.

As illustrated in this model (see figure 1.2) developed by the Collaborative for Academic, Social and Emotional Learning (CASEL), SEL includes both an environmental focus and a person-centered focus (Zins, Weissberg, Wang, and Walberg, 2004). A person-centered focus emphasizes that social and emotional education involves teaching children and adolescents to be self- and socially aware, competent self-managers, and be able to successfully build relationships and make responsible decisions.

SEL instruction is most effective when it is integrated into the school's curriculum and other programs, such as sports and other extracurricular activities, and when it includes meaningful partnerships of schools, families, and communities. Some SEL programs encourage students to use SEL skills to set academic goals and improve their study habits. Other SEL programs infuse SEL skills into academic subject matter, by providing literature activities that require using social awareness to understand a protagonist's motivations and actions (Schonert-Reichl and O'Brien, 2012).

In addition to focusing on specific instruction in social and emotional skills, SEL occurs in the context of a school culture. Therefore, creating a school and classroom community that is caring, supportive, and responsive to

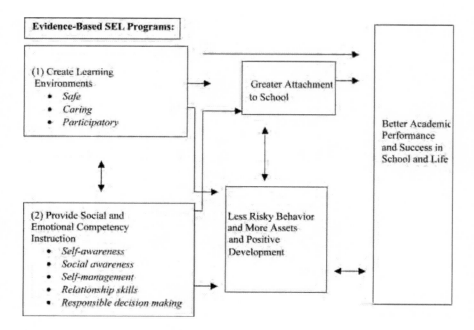

Figure 1.2.   A framework identifying the relations among classroom and school contexts, social and emotional competencies, and outcomes (Schonert-Reichl and O'Brien, 2012, 317).

students' needs is as important as skill instruction and interrelated components in implementing an SEL program at the school level. Based on research that points to the importance of classroom environments (Milkie and Warner, 2011) and positive teacher-student relationships in promoting students' positive social, emotional, and academic competence, the environmental aspect of the model deserves special consideration when we look, next, at school climate (Brackett, Reyes, Rivers, Elbertson, and Salovey, 2011; Jerome, Hamre, and Pianta, 2009).

SCHOOL CLIMATE

> The first step in building safe and supportive schools conducive to academic excellence and student success is to create positive climates. Such climates prevent problem behaviors before they occur and reduce the need for disciplinary interventions that can interfere with student learning. (U.S. Department of Education, 2014, 5)

Over the past few decades, there has been a growing body of empirical research confirming that school climate matters. Positive and sustained school climate is associated with increased academic achievement, positive youth development, effective risk prevention, health promotion efforts, and teacher satisfaction and retention (Adelman and Taylor, 2005; Bryk, Sebring, Allensworth, Luppescu, and Easton, 2010; Centers for Disease Control and Prevention, 2009; Cohen, 2012).

School Climate Defined

School climate refers to the quality and character of school life. Here is how the National School Climate Council (NSCC) defines the concept:

> School climate is based on patterns of people's experience of school life; it reflects the norms, goals, values, interpersonal relationships, teaching, learning, leadership practices, and organizational structures that comprise school life. (National School Climate Council, 2011, 2)

A prosocial school climate embraces the school's mission to create safe, caring, and participatory learning environments. A sustainable, positive school climate fosters the youth development and learning necessary for a productive, contributing, and satisfying life in a democratic society. This climate includes:

- Norms, values, and expectations that support people feeling socially, emotionally, and physically safe.
- People are engaged and respected.

- Students, families, and educators work together to develop, live, and contribute to a shared school vision.
- Educators model and nurture an attitude that emphasizes the benefits and satisfaction from learning.
- Each person contributes to the operations of the school and the care of the physical environment. (National School Climate Council, 2007, 5)

With this in mind, here is my reworking of the central components of a robust school climate as defined by the National School Climate Center (Cohen, 2012).

1. *School climate is an organizing concept.* A core concept in school climate improvement is the importance of recognizing the essential social, emotional, ethical, civic, and intellectual aspects of learning.
2. *A prosocial school climate supports shared leadershi and learning.* A growing body of research and practice calls for education leaders—teachers, principals, and superintendents—to become more transparent about their goals and to ensure that all education stakeholders participate in building a high-quality learning environment (National Middle School Association [NMSA], 2003). Measuring and improving school climate supports transparent, democratically informed leadership and learning (Deal and Peterson, 2009; Kokolis, 2007).
3. *A responsive school climate promotes school-family-community partnerships.* Comprehensive school climate improvement practices should include "the whole village." This means actively seeking meaningful ways of involving parents and other community members in planning and decision-making processes as well as using the school as a center for community activities and services.
4. *A robust school climate promotes student engagement.* There is a growing body of research that underscores the notion that when students are engaged in meaningful learning and work (e.g., in service-learning), the result is that achievement, positive youth development, and school connectedness are all enhanced. When students become involved in the process of developing, implementing, and understanding change projects that grow out of their analysis of school and community needs, we are promoting the skills and dispositions that support engaged citizenry and student engagement in particular (Cohen, 2006; Kohlberg and Higgins, 1987; Reed, 2008).
5. *School climate improvement is an on-going process.* Schools are not static institutions. Students and staff are continually changing, as are the demands on public education and the socioeconomic conditions that influence school politics, challenges, and resources. School climate improvement requires a set of reflective steps that include use of

a valid assessment, stake-holder involvement in reviewing climate data from multiple sources, and planning for programs and services in response to those data and student needs.

The National School Climate Council (2011) has developed a set of standards based on these principles (see www.schoolclimate.org/climate/documents) that have been endorsed by a number of national organizations and that have proven useful to school districts and state-level planners as well.

School Climate Policy

Policymakers need to become more aware of school climate research and the importance of a positive school climate in determining academic success. There are compelling reasons why K–12 schools need to evaluate school climate in scientifically sound ways and use these findings to create a climate for learning.

For example, prosocial school climate can significantly impact graduation rates. A large study of 276 Virginia high schools found that a school climate characterized by lower rates of bullying and teasing was predictive of higher graduation rates four years later. Even more impressive was the study's finding that having a problematic school climate was as important a factor in failing to graduate from high school as was student poverty (Cornell, Gregory, Huang, and Fan, 2013).

National, state, and local district policies on school climate should:

1. Define school climate in ways that are aligned with recent research;
2. Recommend that schools routinely evaluate school climate comprehensively, recognizing student, parent, and school personnel "voice" and that it is necessary to assess all of the major dimensions (e.g., safety, relationships, teaching and learning, and the environment) that shape school climate;
3. Consider adopting or adapting the National School Climate Standards (http://schoolclimate.org/climate/standards.php) that reflect and suggest norms and values that support democratically informed learning, teaching, and school improvement efforts;
4. Use school climate assessment as a measure of accountability;
5. Ensure that credential options maintain high-quality school climate–related standards for educators and school-based mental health professionals in general, and administrators in particular;
6. Encourage teacher preparation programs that give teachers and administrators the tools to evaluate classroom and school climate and take steps to use these findings to promote a climate for learning and development in our schools; and

7. Increase support for research on the evaluation and improvement of school climate.

School Climate Policy Example

The Westbrook, Connecticut, Board of Education (2014) adopted a school climate policy based on the NSCC standards. It includes the legal context for the standards, a rich set of definitions, specific guidelines for district-wide, and school-level implementation of a rigorous process of continuous school climate improvement. The following section of the policy delineates the planning process that pulls together the roles and responsibilities of all the players in the school community who have a stake in creating a prosocial school climate, as well as the actions that the school board believes will create a foundation for continued improvement:

VII. School Climate Improvement Plans:

1. In collaboration with the [district] Coordinator, each [school] Specialist shall develop and/or update an Improvement Plan based on the findings of the School Climate Survey.
2. The Specialist and the Committee shall develop and/or update the Improvement Plan, using the School Climate Improvement Plan template (Appendix C), taking into consideration the needs of all key stakeholders, with sensitivity to equity and diversity.

The Improvement Plan shall support the actualization of the following five Standards:

Standard 1: Develop a **shared vision** and plan for promoting, enhancing and sustaining a positive school climate.

Standard 2: Develop **policies** that promote social, emotional, ethical, civic and intellectual learning as well as systems that address barriers to learning.

Standard 3: Implement **practices** that promote the learning and positive social, emotional, ethical and civic development of students and student engagement as well as addressing barriers to learning.

Standard 4: Create an environment where all members are **welcomed, supported, and feel safe** in school: socially, emotionally, intellectually and physically.

Standard 5: Develop meaningful and engaging practices, activities and norms that promote social and civic responsibilities and a commitment to social justice.

Each Improvement Plan shall be submitted to the Coordinator for approval and implementation no later than mid-September of each school year. The

Coordinator may provide feedback to the Committee with respect to amendments to the Improvement Plan. (Westbrook, Connecticut, 2014, 8)

FIVE THINGS YOU SHOULD KNOW
ABOUT SCHOOL DISCIPLINE

A recent issue of *Child Trends* (Darling-Churchill, 2014) provides a useful overview of the key points emphasized throughout this book at the core of the movement to reform disciplinary policy and practices:

1. *School discipline actions should be considered as learning opportunities rather than measures to keep order and enable academics to proceed.* Though often viewed through a negative lens as managing student behavior, school personnel, families, and other student support services can work together to use disciplinary matters to support positive child and youth development and ensure school success.
2. *Student behavior problems may be about more than the behavior itself.* Student disciplinary infractions may reflect students' struggles with increasingly rigorous academic expectations, or circumstances affecting them outside of school. While behavior issues, absenteeism, and violence in schools undeniably impact academic instruction, policies, and disciplinary actions that fail to consider the range of student backgrounds and contexts are missing an opportunity to identify needed supports for at-risk and struggling students.
3. *Research shows a strong link between disciplinary policies and actions and a host of negative outcomes.* Suspension in ninth grade doubles a student's likelihood of dropping out, from 16 percent to 32 percent for those suspended just once, and students with a history of disciplinary issues are at risk of ending up entangled in the criminal justice system. Nonpunitive responses to negative behaviors (such as targeted behavioral supports) have shown promise in reducing violent behavior in school.
4. *Recent federal guidance supports efforts to ensure that discipline practices are fair and equitable.* In response to evidence of the uneven application of school discipline practices based on race, ethnicity, gender, or other characteristics—known as "disproportionality"—the Department of Education is encouraging schools and districts to develop research-based, locally tailored approaches to discipline that strive to circumvent exclusionary discipline, especially for minor misbehaviors. Many school systems are embracing this opportunity to showcase or accelerate their progress in this area.

5. *Schools set the tone for the disciplinary climate.* Thoughtfully designed and administered school discipline policies can serve to maintain safety and order, while also providing supports for students. Encouraging positive relationships between students and adults, promoting students' sense of belonging, having student supports available,
and training staff on classroom management are at the core of positive
school climates and solution-focused disciplinary environments, and
can minimize the need to resort to harsher school discipline.

SUMMING UP

The foundation for a safe school rests on the creation of a healthy school
climate, a caring community where students feel safe and secure. There are
two main conditions which facilitate and support safety and security:

1. An orderly, predictable environment where school staff provide consistent, reliable supervision and discipline in the context of a culture
where prosocial values are articulated and lived, and
2. A school climate where students feel connected to the school and
respected and supported by their teachers and other school staff.

A balance of structure and support is essential, and requires an organized,
school-wide approach that is practiced by all school personnel (Brown, Corrigan, and D'Alessandro, 2012; Sugai and Horner, 2008; Mayer, 1995).

Being a somebody, having an identity in school, means being accepted as
part of a group, in the classroom and with other students. This is why social
belonging is such a key feature of programs highlighted in this volume.
Strategies and approaches such as social-emotional learning and restorative
justice have shown success in building positive school climates where children spend their energy contributing to the greater good rather than defending themselves from bullying and other forms of aggression and violence.

The effectiveness of the rules and sanctions that form the public outline of
discipline policies are mediated by both the actual interactions of all of the
school community members and how they are perceived. Beyond teaching
the five core SEL competencies, efforts to create a prosocial school climate
must also include a focus on adult relationships, and an emphasis on adult
modeling of appropriate behaviors. The quality of interactions between all
members of the school community constitute a "hidden curriculum" that
defines the moral fiber of a school. School discipline rests in the web of this
hidden curriculum.

Chapter Two

Developing and Revising a Code of Student Conduct to Support Your School Mission and Improve Your School Climate

Philip M. Brown

Virtually every pre-K–12 school in the country has some version of a code of student conduct (CSC). The traditional purpose of the school's CSC is to (1) outline in general terms the kind of behavior that is expected of students (and sometimes adults) in the school setting, (2) identify the specific behaviors that are proscribed and that the school district has determined are not permitted, and (3) alert students and parents to the consequences when proscribed behaviors are violated, along with an accompanying list of penalties for violations.

Code of conduct violations typically include relatively common or minor infractions such as tardiness, use of foul or obscene language, failure to comply with dress code, and more recently inappropriate cell phone use. They also include the penalties for more extreme or disruptive behaviors such as fighting, persistent bullying, and harassment, some of which can rise to the level of serious crimes.

The CSC is usually provided as a handbook in hard copy form as part of a back-to-school package distributed to students and their parents/guardians, as well as school staff. More robust school Web sites make a digital version available online. In larger districts, the CSC is sometimes also translated for students and families whose first language is not English. Some more sophisticated CSCs also include behavioral expectations for teachers and parents, alerting the entire school community to its contribution to maintaining an environment conducive to learning.

This chapter explores the usually unrealized potential the CSC has for establishing and supporting a positive, developmentally sound approach to student discipline and school climate. It is often recommended that school districts and schools review the CSC on an annual basis and make adjustments to keep it up to date. However, the approach taken here requires a much more fundamental reexamination of the revision process that can result in:

- More open communication with parents, students, and staff;
- A values-based CSC that supports the development of moral reasoning, ethical behavior, and the mission statement of the school system;
- A clear explanation of the relationship between preventive programs (such as instruction in social, emotional skills), student support services (such as peer support groups or counseling), and the desired school culture and climate;
- A more consistent and meaningful disciplinary system that supports positive student development rather than relying on punitive consequences to affect behavior; and
- Why you should consider revising and enhancing your CSC, who should be involved, and what issues and outcomes you can expect.

Much of the information in this chapter reflects what was learned from a pilot study in three New Jersey school districts that implemented the process recommended here over a two-year period beginning in 2007, which was part of a grant from the U.S. Department of Education to the New Jersey Department of Education.

REVIEWING AND REVISING YOUR CODE OF STUDENT CONDUCT

The process outlined in this chapter begins with a fundamental proposition: revising your CSC should be a significant endeavor involving many members of the school community, not a bureaucratic exercise. The reason for spending the time and energy required in this process is that the CSC can serve many important purposes. It reviews district and school policies, sets the tone for school culture and climate, serves as a roadmap for student (and we suggest, staff and parent) behaviors that impact everyday school life, and provides a reliable and objective source of information for all members of the school community.

What follows explores the purpose of the CSC, and invites readers to ask important questions about the status of their current CSC: How is it used now? Who created it and when? What is the current status of staff, student, and parent satisfaction with the existing discipline system, and how can this process identify and address changes you want to make?

The process outlined here assumes that CSCs are generally established at the school district level for public schools and need approval from the governing body for both public and private or charter schools. For reasons that will become apparent, it is important to have an identified team to conduct the review and revisions of the CSC, which at various times in the process should include school-level leaders (principals, teachers, and support staff), students, parents, and even community members.

Defining Our Terms: What Does It Mean to Have a Code of Student Conduct?

A *code* is a law or rule, and also a way of converting information from one source to another. Think of Morse code, used for years as a way to reliably convert language into electrical signals and back into language. The CSC serves both as a set of rules and a way of transmitting crucial policy and procedural information about school rules to members of the school community.

Conduct refers to our deportment or how we direct, control, and manage ourselves. All members of the school community need to have information about behavioral expectations and conduct stated clearly. Without agreed upon guidelines for conduct, both explicit and implicit, our social lives would be chaotic at best, and likely dangerous as well. Think of the last time you were in a school where violence was a daily occurrence and armed police were visibly present.

Wikipedia ("code of conduct," n.d.) provides an instructive working definition of a *code of conduct* for organizations developed by the International Federation of Accountants: "Principals, values, standards, or rules of behavior that guide the decisions, procedures and systems of an organization in a way that (a) contributes to the welfare of its key stakeholders, and (b) respects the rights of all constituents affected by its operations."

This is a useful definition if we ask ourselves the following question: In schools, who are the key stakeholders whose welfare is important? While the *S* in CSC focuses on student conduct, it is immediately clear that school staff, parents, and the welfare of the community are all impacted by student conduct. It also suggests that behavioral expectations should be included for all of these members of the school community. If only all of the accountants who worked for Enron, major banks, and financial institutions could have acted in accordance with this definition, think of the hurt our country would have been saved!

What Purpose Does Your Current CSC Serve?

As you begin, ask yourself and your team the following questions and discuss the implications for your plan to revise your school/district CSC:

- Is your CSC required by state law or regulation? (See the example below.)
- Is there one district-level CSC? What latitude do individual schools have to formulate or tweak their own CSCs?
- Historically, who was involved in the development of your current CSC? When was it last revised?
- If you asked teachers, students, and parents what the purpose of the CSC is, what do believe they would say?

Example: Regulatory Requirement for Developing the CSC

The New Jersey State Board of Education developed regulations governing CSCs that signaled a shift from a focus on student behavior problems and disciplinary consequences (necessary though they are) to a focus on positive student development. Here are the goals they espoused. The purpose of the CSC should be to:

1. Foster the health, safety, and social and emotional well-being of students;
2. Support the establishment and maintenance of civil, safe, secure, supportive, and disciplined school environments conducive to learning;
3. Promote achievement of high academic standards;
4. Prevent the occurrence of problem behaviors;
5. Establish parameters for the intervention and remediation of student problem behaviors at all stages of identification; and
6. Establish parameters for school responses to violations of the CSC that take into account, the severity of the offenses, the developmental ages of the student offenders and students' histories of inappropriate behaviors.

(N.J.A.C 6A: 16–7., n.d)

Defining the purpose of your CSC provides an opportunity to look deeply at the school's role as the primary public institution to which our society has given the responsibility of socializing young people to their role as citizens. Schools can serve as models of our democratic institutions and how they should function, just as teachers and other adults who work in schools serve as role models for behavior and good character. How does your school support this vision of the school and staff roles? If it does not, what are the implications?

Why Revise Your School District/School CSC?

Consider the issues that may drive your need to revise your CSC:

- No relation between district/school mission statement and the current CSC. Check to see that the school/district core values discussed later in this chapter are present in the mission statement.
- An outmoded, punitive disciplinary framework; no positive behaviors or expectations.
- Inadequate presentation of harassment, intimidation, and bullying behaviors and consequences.
- Inconsistencies in behavior standards and how similar rule infractions are handled between buildings (e.g., is a violation of the dress code treated the same way in two middle schools in the same district?).
- Disparities in how discipline is meted out between teachers and administrators in different schools in the same district.
- Disparities in how discipline is handled in responding to the same behaviors by different racial or ethnic groups.
- Data showing deteriorating discipline, absenteeism, and complaints by students and parents.

When school administrators contemplate the revision process, it is crucial to begin with a wide-eyed look at the status of your system and the reasons that cause you to need to move ahead. Starting in a defensive position inevitably leads to forming a process that excludes voices that may have important, if disturbing, information to provide.

In one of the districts involved in the pilot study, because the superintendent was wise enough to include both parents and community representatives recommended by the elected township officials, he learned things that would otherwise never have come to light. Parents recommended that many recent immigrant families in the district needed to understand the basic parameters and expectations of American public education—there was no reason to expect that they understood their annual four-week trip back to India in the middle of the year created problems for their children's teacher.

The context for developing your CSC is the desire to create a civil school climate that supports the moral and ethical development of children. The purpose of the CSC is to create a sound basis for a positive, civil school climate, not just a set of rules and consequences to govern behavior. The CSC should be based on parent, student, and community involvement that represents, where possible, the composition of the schools and community.

INITIAL STEPS IN PREPARING TO REVISE THE CSC

As with any changes in school policy and procedures, planning is key to success. The following are factors to consider before and during the initial phases of the revision process. In the New Jersey pilot the entire revision took each district more than a year to accomplish—longer than we anticipated—but all three districts agreed in the end that it was time well spent.

1. Get backing from the superintendent, principal, headmaster, and board of education. Leadership is critical to a successful process, especially because you will face potential controversies and differences of opinion where consensus is desirable and tough decisions necessary.
2. Be able to articulate your rationale. Review the issues listed previously and be able to clearly describe the reasons for the contemplated revisions.
3. Set the stage early for the involvement of parents, community representatives, students, and staff in different phases of the process.
4. Form a school- or district-level project team that will guide and stick with the process. Make sure that your team factors in adequate representation from, and support for, building principals throughout the process. Elementary and secondary principals have different interests and concerns. If it is a large district, you may need separate committees for elementary and secondary levels.
5. The CSC should define student behavioral expectations in terms that support core ethical values (the next section is devoted to the creation of school core ethical values).
6. The CSC should include the school/district's curricular and co-curricular methods of instruction aimed at social-emotional skill development and support for a prosocial school climate. For example, conduct an inventory of the social and life-skill development programs currently being used throughout the district's schools. Are they articulated across grade levels so that learning is scaffolded and skills reinforced, or are there uncoordinated programs with skill presentations that may confuse or bore students? This could be a separate process that will have implications for curriculum articulation and providing information that should be integrated into or linked to the CSC.

7. Provide feedback to all of the stakeholders involved as resolution is reached at critical steps in the project plan. For example, keep the PTA/PTO as well as board members apprised of progress being made by including their members in the process and updating them through school-district communications such as newsletters or a special section of the district Web site.
8. Communicate the CSC clearly through student handbooks translated, if necessary, into the primary languages of students' home cultures.
9. Provide for a positive presentation to the school board prior to formal adoption of a new or revised CSC, using support from stakeholders involved in its development.
10. Include a provision for annual updating of the CSC, based on feedback from school staff, students, and other stakeholders.

Establishing Core Ethical Values as the Basis for Codes of Student Conduct

Establishing core ethical and performance values with associated behaviors for all members of the school community sets expectations that can reinforce positive assets and transform negative aspects of school culture (Lickona and Davidson, 2005; Brown and Sapora-Day, 2008). Core ethical values enable us to treat each other with fairness, respect, and care, and ensure that we pursue our performance goals in ethical rather than unethical ways.

Performance values, in turn, enable us to act on our ethical values and make a positive difference in the world. We take initiative to right a wrong or be of service to others; we persevere to overcome problems and mend relationships. Performance values can be chosen and treated the same way as the core ethical values exercises, and are more important for academic success, but less for conduct or behavior. (To learn more about performance values go to http://www.character.org/key-topics/what-is-character-education/performance-values.)

Core ethical values should function as the foundation for rules of conduct and serve as the unifying thread for your CSC. Why? A CSC that does not espouse the values it is based on lacks the moral authority that defines the reasons for requiring rules at all. The CSC establishes the school/district's unwavering commitment to use these values as the reference point for decision-making regarding behavior of all members of the school community.

As developmental psychologist and educator Larry Nucci points out, it is important to establish school rules carefully because "Schools and classrooms are mini-societies governed by moral rules and conventional norms. An important way in which school contributes to children's social and moral development is how rules and norms are established and enforced" (2009, 66).

The following process used to establish core values was liberally adapted from what is recommended by the Character Education Partnership and defined in their *Eleven Principles Sourcebook* (Beland, 2003). The *Sourcebook* defines values and core ethical values as follows: "A value is a belief about what is good that transcends a specific situation and that guides judgment and decision making (Rokeach, 1973). In order for a value to be a 'core ethical value' it must be of central importance in the life of the individual and life of the community" (Beland, 2003, 5).

Core ethical values must have all of the following characteristics:

- Universal. (They must apply to all people; all should live this way ideally.)
- Moral and ethical in nature. (They should deal with issues of right and wrong, not personal preferences, tastes, or opinions.)
- Supportive of our democracy and democratic way of life. (They should be consistent with how a good citizen should act.)
- Affirming and supportive of every individual. (They should affirm our human dignity and fundamental human rights.)
- Important to relationships. (They should function as behaviors that support and reaffirm the Golden Rule.)
- Important to decision making. (They assist us in making the right decisions in everyday interactions and in difficult situations.)
- Significant, rather than trivial. (They inform and affect the most important parts of our lives.) (Beland, 2003, Principle 1).

The Montvale, New Jersey, school district used a process consistent with the outline in the *Sourcebook* with a large representative group of school staff, a parent/community group, and eighth-grade students in their health classes to arrive at a consensus regarding their core ethical values. This is the two-part process they used with each group:

Identifying Important Core Ethical Values

Part I: Choosing Your Values through Dialogue and Consensus

- Begin by introducing the definition of core ethical values and their characteristics (see previous text). Because this is unfamiliar territory for many, ask for examples of values that are not core ethical values but are significant for children (e.g., having the right clothes, going on a vacation to Disneyland, having the newest video game).
- Break the group into table teams of about five to eight people. Select a table leader/recorder.

- Use the following process to identify each group's core values:

  1. Each individual lists the core values that they believe would be the most important for their students and school community. What are the values we want to live by?
  2. Each team member shares his or her list, indicating why they selected the values they did. The table leader makes a combined list, noting which values received multiple mentions.
  3. Through group discussion, speak for/against each item on the list. Why does each selected value have relevance for your school, your students, your life? Are they truly core ethical values or just preferences?
  4. The table team arrives at consensus of their top three or four choices and the leader presents their choices to the whole group.
  5. As each table group presents its choices, create a new master list on a white board or chart paper, again making a combined list, noting which values received multiple mentions.
  6. The exercise leader may need to eliminate or redefine table group choices if they have chosen values that are not core ethical values (e.g., punctuality or thinking clearly). Test this list against the characteristics for core ethical values.
  7. Discuss how many of the core ethical values on your posted list your school cannot live without, are so important that you want to keep them as the basis for school rules.

- You now have a provisional list of core ethical values. If the original group is not representative of your school community, this same process should be repeated with different subgroups (staff, parents, community representatives, students [sixth grade and up or student councils]), and a final consensus reached regarding the district/school's core ethical values.

Part II: Defining Core Ethical Values Behaviorally

- Core ethical values do not have clear and significant meaning unless they are defined in behavioral terms. This exercise is the first step leading to an understanding of what the selected core ethical values mean and how they can be used practically to guide student (and staff) behavior. It breathes life into the virtues represented by the values.

1. Begin with a staff group or table teams as with Part I. Ask the group to create a behavioral definition for each of your selected core ethical values. Begin by having each group construct a *T-chart* with the core value written at the top, and to the left side of the T write examples of specific behaviors that uphold or are in accord with and exemplify the value.

2. Be concrete. For example, how do staff demonstrate respect for students? For each other? What does the value look like? How do I know it when I see someone doing it? What does the value sound like when I hear someone say things that affirm or support it?

3. On the right side of the T-chart repeat the process using negative examples rather than positive ones. What does it look like and sound like when someone is behaving in a way that does not support the value?

4. When this exercise is done with some openness and encouragement, it frequently leads staff to begin identifying what Roland Barth calls "the nondiscussables"; the subjects that are so laden with anxiety and fearfulness that they do not get dealt with in faculty meetings or formal interactions, but cause considerable toxicity to the school culture (Barth, 2002). If this happens, be prepared to use this work to look at how the school or district can address climate issues as well, using the CSC as a significant tool. See chapter 1 for more on school climate.

• Using the results of this exercise, your staff committee is now in a position to draft definitions for the core ethical values.

Using the Core Ethical Values as the Basis for
Enhancing Student Discipline Procedures

Once your school district/school's core ethical values have been agreed upon, there are two uses for them that related directly to student discipline at both the classroom and school levels. At the school level, the core ethical values can be used as a part of the disciplinary referral procedure. Here is the form that Hunterdon Central High School in New Jersey developed to do that:

HUNTERDON CENTRAL REGIONAL HIGH SCHOOL
CODE OF CONDUCT REPORT

STUDENT NAME._____ 9 101112 TODAY'S DATE._____

_____ REPORTING STAFF __DATE

OF INCIDENT_____BLOCK

Dear Parent/Guardian: The Code of Conduct at HCRHS is based on the following pillars of character. The check mark indicates the pillar that was breached. A brief description and applicable consequences are listed below. Please assist us in helping your child understand the implications of their actions and accept the related consequences.

CARING: I will be sensitive to the beliefs, ideas, feelings and experiences of others.

CITIZENSHIP: I will take pride and be a role model in my country, my town and my school.

FAIRNESS: I will treat others equally regardless of their ideas, opinions or moral standards.

RESPECT: I will be considerate of the feelings and property of others and treat them without bias or judgment

RESPONSIBILITY: I will act in a mature manner and be prepared for any consequences both positive and negative.

TRUSTWORTHINESS: I will be reliable, honest and dependable.

Reason for Referral:

___Excessive Tardiness to Class/School	___Substance Abuse Violation	___ Parking Violation
___ Destruction to School Property	___ Smoking/Possession of Tobacco Products	___Theft
___ Class Cutting	___Insubordination/Uncooperative Behavior	___ Abusive Language
___Dress Code Violation	___ Use of Electronic Device	___Disruptive Behavior
___Computer Infraction	___ Loitering/Off Limits	___ID Violation
___Fighting	___ Reassignment of Discipline	___Truancy
___Bus Misconduct	___Cafeteria Misconduct	

Description

_____

Staff Action Prior to Referral:

___Conference with Student	___Consulted Department Chair	___Teacher Detention
___Consulted Counselor/VP	___Behavioral Intervention	___Removed Student from Class
___ Previous Warning	___Parent Contact	

Figure 2.1. Hunterdon Central Regional High School code of conduct report and praise referral.

Other: _____

Administrative Action: House Detention date(s) _____ Saturday Detention date(s) _____

In School Suspension _____ Out of School Suspension _____

Other: _____

Administrator: _____

Notice that this is a form that is used by staff in referring a student to the vice-principal and it is produced as a snap set, so that one copy goes home to the student's parent as well. There is a parallel form using the same core values definitions that is used by the staff to recognize students for positive behavior, which looks like this:

HUNTERDON CENTRAL REGIONAL HIGH SCHOOL
PRAISE REFERRAL

Student Name _____ **ID #** _____ **Grade**____

Reporting Teacher _____**Date** _____

Dear Parent/Guardian: The Code of Conduct at HCRHS is based on the following pillars of character. The check mark indicates the pillar that was breached. A brief description and applicable consequences are listed below. Please assist us in helping your child understand the implications of their actions and accept the related consequences.

CARING: I will be sensitive to the beliefs, ideas, feelings and experiences of others.

CITIZENSHIP: I will take pride and be a role model in my country, my town and my school.

FAIRNESS: I will treat others equally regardless of their ideas, opinions or moral standards.

RESPECT: I will be considerate of the feelings and property of others and treat them without bias or judgment

RESPONSIBILITY: I will act in a mature manner and be prepared for any consequences both positive and negative.

TRUSTWORTHINESS: I will be reliable, honest and dependable.

REASON FOR REFERRAL

ACADEMICS:
____ Excellent job on
a major project __ Timely assignments ___Academic improvement
___Improved __Attends tutorial __High quality assignments
participation __Contributes significantly
in class
_____

Other: _____

PERSONAL BEHAVIOR: __Proacti pressure well
__Improved class behavior ve __School spirit
__Less tardy __ __Extracurricular achievement
_Shows respect for others Handles __ Volunteer work
__Emphasizes the positive __Other

Figure 2.1 *(cont.)*. Hunterdon Central Regional High School code of conduct report and praise referral.

SCHOOL COMMUNITY SUPPORT:

__Helps maintain school's physical appearance	__Kind/warm	__Consistent attendance
__Achievement outside of school	__Responsive to others	__Motivates others
__Community Service	__Courteous	__Cooperative
Other:	__Helpful to all	__Honest
	__Enthusiastic	__Conscientious
	__ Sense of humor	__Handles pressure well

_____

_____

ADDITIONAL COMMENTS:

_____

_____

_____

Administrator   _____

Figure 2.1 *(cont.)*. Hunterdon Central Regional High School code of conduct report and praise referral.

The power of using core ethical values is not limited to the CSC. They can be infused into the curriculum at all levels, used as the basis for creative games and recognition practices that can truly turn a school into a national model. See the Character Education Partnerships National Schools of Character Program for scores of examples of how schools have transformed their culture by using the core ethical values in just these ways (http://www.character.org).

Performance Values

Performance values enable us to act on our ethical values and make a positive difference in the world, and create a school culture of excellence where love of learning, work that matters, and acceptance of feedback thrive. Examples of performance values are creativity, persistence, curiosity, diligence, collaboration, and self-discipline. In choosing core values that will guide a district/school to its true goals, both core ethical and performance values are appropriate and necessary.

Core ethical and performance values function in complementary ways. For example, a successful professional learning community requires self-discipline (performance value) to keep to an agenda and a sense of responsibility (core ethical value) to the group for active participation. The same process outlined previously can be used to generate performance values, but because there is less emphasis and understanding of core ethical values it is strongly recommended that they be kept separate processes.

Reviewing Your Existing Code of Student Conduct: Issues to Keep in Mind

Define the Expectations for Appropriate, Prosocial Behavior for the Entire School Community

The first step is defining core ethical values with examples of behaviors for students of different age and developmental levels, as well as for adults, as indicated previously. At the classroom level, use the T-chart exercise on page 30 at the beginning of the school year when establishing rules and have students list examples of the kinds of behaviors that exemplify the core value: "What does it look and sound like when we are being respectful?" This provides a sound basis for communicating and reinforcing expectations for positive student behavior throughout the year, and can be modified and used for students at all grade levels.

Articulating expectations for adult conduct and positive interactions with youth is especially important. Here is the list of staff expectations that the Cherry Hill school district in New Jersey outlined in its CSC (Cherry Hill School District, 2009, 3).

The school staff is expected to:

- Model positive modes of behavior and good manners.
- Exercise respect and civility in all interactions with staff, students, and members of the community.
- Maintain a positive learning environment during the school day.
- Explain and discuss acceptable and unacceptable modes of behavior with students and parents/guardians.
- Foster an emphasis on positive behaviors creating an atmosphere of mutual respect and the appreciation of individual differences among staff, students, and parents for individuals as well as for district and community property.
- Inform and enforce the discipline structure with students.
- Be consistent in enforcing the discipline structure throughout the school.
- Comply with requirements of New Jersey Administrative Code and District policies and procedures.

Graded Response to Conduct Problems and the Developmental Appropriateness of Sanctions

As you discuss the consequences of different violations of the defined behavioral expectations, it is important to keep in mind that the responses are graded according to:

- The severity of the offense.

- The developmental ages and level of the student offenders.
- The students' histories of inappropriate behaviors.
- The student's and victim's special circumstances and needs.

The goal should be to keep students in school whenever possible, limiting the use of out-of-school suspensions and expulsions to the most serious offenses. Also keep in mind that for students with disabilities, attendance, punitive, and remedial procedures are applied in accordance with the Individual Educational Plan. The CSC should also make clear how the district/school will interact with law enforcement in addressing delinquent acts that are more serious in nature such as vandalism, theft, and violence, as well as status offenses such a chronic truancy or curfew violations.

Consider What Programs Are Currently in Place in
Your District/School That Could Support the Prevention and
Intervention Components of Your CSC

When was the last time you reviewed the current programs and student services that support the effort to promote positive youth development? This is a good time to identify gaps in the programs and services that may be indicated through the review process or as a result of other indicators such as discipline incidents or a school climate assessment. Describe strategies to support positive behavior of all students, including youth with intensive behavioral health needs. As the recently released School Discipline Consensus Report (Morgan, Salomon, Plotkin, and Cohen, 2014, 79) puts it well: "Many incidents of misconduct are the result of students' lack of social and emotional skills, so infractions or disruptions should be considered not just as a disciplinary matter, but also in the context of the youths' development."

How can instruction and special programs be brought into better alignment with the CSC, and are there new initiatives that should be considered to facilitate the impact of the CSC on school culture and climate? This part of your revisions effort can be separately conducted, but should be integrated into the framework when you roll out revisions to your CSC. In doing such a review remember to include staff familiar with curriculum and instruction as well as representatives from helping services from the school and community, such as school-based health and mental health services.

Table 2.1 shows how one of the school districts in the New Jersey pilot project showed alignment between their core ethical values and the skills taught in their curriculum through the Social Decision-Making and Problem Solving program (Highland Park School District, 2009).

School District and School Building Level Documents

Traditionally, it is through the school or student handbooks provided in the beginning of each academic year that students and parents are informed of student behavioral expectations and consequences. In large or decentralized school district systems, or where principals have considerable discretion in publishing their school's student handbook, it is not uncommon for there to be significant discrepancies in the rules of conduct and related consequences as well as differences in format and general content.

School systems need to have consistency across school buildings for students of common developmental or grade levels. In one of the pilot districts, there were nineteen buildings and nineteen different student handbooks. It took several meetings of principals at each level (elementary, middle, and high school) to reach agreement on how to create an agreed upon framework and content for their CSCs, while allowing for a measure of separate identity for each school.

Is Your Current Mission Statement Consistent with
Your Proposed Core Ethical Values?

Check to see when your mission statement was adopted. Revising your district/school mission statement at the same time you are revising your CSC is a wise move because it is an opportunity to reinforce the importance of your core values and articulate the importance of whole child development as well as academic success.

Make the Approval Process for a Revised CSC Part of Your Plan

In public school districts and in private and charter schools, a governance board needs to approve the CSC. As you plan your revisions, consider how and when the plan, a draft, and final version will be submitted to them for review and approval. Also consider if a draft needs to be submitted so that the decision-makers have an opportunity for reaction or input before you ask

Table 2.1.   Aligning core values and SEL skills.

Core Ethical Value	Skill Set
Respect	Speaker Power
Responsibility	Listening Skills
Caring	Class Meetings/Self-Awareness
Courage	Feelings Expression/Self-Awareness
Social Harmony	Keep Calm/Emotional Regulation
	B.E.S.T./Effective Communication
	Hassle Logging/Decision Making

them to vote on or agree to it. If there will be a formal, public presentation of the revised CSC, make sure that those stakeholders who were instrumental in its creation are there to both support it and receive credit, and assist in answering questions if necessary.

Don't Underestimate the Power of Public Approval and Support

It is important to take full advantage of the formal act of adoption of the revised CSC by disseminating it well and making it clear that the school/district commitment to it is real and strong. In addition to dissemination through vehicles such as the student handbook, which typically goes to parents and students at the beginning of the school year, make sure the CSC is prominent and accessible through your Web site. You should check and decide if the CSC needs to be translated into any of the primary languages used at home by non-English speaking parents.

Here is the way the Cherry Hill School District (which has been honored with a number of National Schools of Character awards) begins its finalized CSCs after almost two years of revision work (Cherry Hill Public Schools, 2009, introductory page):

CODE OF STUDENT CONDUCT
CHERRY HILL PUBLIC SCHOOLS

October 2009

Dear Students, Parents and Guardians:

Because who we are as individuals makes up what we are together, whether family, school, community, or nation, we have established the following character traits as an overall framework for our district and our schools. We know that we all learn best and most fully in an atmosphere where the opinions and rights of all are honored and respected. Therefore, our core values are:

Respect: The student demonstrates an understanding of respectful behavior, and conducts himself/herself in a respectful manner.

Responsibility: The student demonstrates an understanding of responsible behavior, and conducts himself/herself in a responsible manner.

Citizenship: The student demonstrates an understanding of the importance of knowing and practicing the values, beliefs, and principles fundamental to participation in the United States' constitutional democracy.

We believe in your potential, your ability to learn, the talents you have to share, and the contribution you can make to our schools and to our future as a nation. The following sections will further outline our most important guidelines for making your school life most productive and positive.

David Campbell, Ed.D., Superintendent

SUMMING UP

A code of student conduct should be envisioned as the key document that sets the tone for social relationships and behavioral expectations. It can serve as a potent tool in providing for a supportive and safe school climate and culture. To serve this purpose it must:

- Be based on the school district and school mission statement, which includes consensually agreed upon core ethical and performance values.
- Have input from all critical school-community partners.
- Speak to parent and staff as well as student behavioral expectations.
- Emphasize student development opportunities, not only punitive consequences.
- Summarize or refer to other publicly available documents that summarize the prosocial instructional and extracurricular programs and activities that support the core ethical and performance values.
- Be made a living document through its utilization and continual updating.

Chapter Three

Systemic Approaches

THE ACHIEVING WITH INTEGRITY PROJECT: POSITIVE
APPROACHES TO DEALING WITH ACADEMIC DISHONESTY

Jason M. Stephens and David B. Wangaard

High school educators in the United States must face the unmet disciplinary challenge of academic dishonesty. The problem of cheating reached epidemic proportions decades ago (e.g., Schab, 1991), yet relatively little has been done to ameliorate it. Particularly rare are positive approaches to promoting academic honesty; that is, programs designed to equip students with the "developmental assets" (Benson, Scales, Hamilton, and Sesma, 2006) needed to achieve with integrity.

Philosophically, positive youth development approaches (e.g., Berkowitz, Sherblom, Bier, and Battistich, 2006; Damon, 2004) stand in stark contrast to behavioristic "police and punish" approaches. The former seek to develop the person through the educational experiences (providing opportunities for students to learn and grow) while the latter seek to control the behavior through environmental contingencies (usually in the form of punishment for the commission of proscribed behaviors).

At present, it is the latter type of approaches that seem be the most commonplace, particularly in high schools. While such approaches might be necessary (i.e., schools need to have clear policies against cheating and equally clear consequences for their violation), they are not sufficient. Not only has police and punish failed to stem the spread of cheating over the past several decades, these strategies fall short in their scope—narrowly focusing on deterrence through threat of punishment, and ignoring the possibility of prevention through promotion of positive developmental assets such as greater ethical awareness, judgment, and commitment related to academic integrity.

This chapter focuses on the *Achieving with Integrity* Project, offering a brief summary of the two programs developed within this project over the past decade. The first program involves a school-wide approach to promote academic integrity, while the second program offers a classroom-level approach to improve student ethical functioning.

Both programs have been described in greater detail elsewhere (Stephens and Wangaard, in press; Wangaard and Stephens, 2011), so the goal of this chapter is to overview them in brief and provide more practical information concerning their adoption and implementation. In doing so, this chapter hopes to offer educational leaders more positive approaches to dealing with academic dishonesty, and aid them in turning the epidemic of cheating into an opportunity for positive ethical development in youth.

Background of the *Achieving with Integrity* Project

The *Achieving with Integrity* (AwI) Project began in 2006, when Stephens and Wangaard started working together on the problem of academic cheating. Both saw the problem as a troubling and unrelenting epidemic in need of more comprehensive and positive approaches. With the support of the John Templeton Foundation and other funders, the authors created two distinct programs aimed at filling that need: one involving school-wide approaches and other classroom-level discussions. This section of the chapter describes the purposes and scope of each program.

Before turning to those descriptions, it is important to note that the two programs were designed to complement one another—each offering a unique set of interventions at a distinct level of school organization; together producing a multilevel approach. However, despite the obvious synergies of implementing both programs, each can stand alone and work on its own.

School-wide Approach: Creating a Culture of Academic Integrity

The first program of the AwI Project was developed based on the premise that a comprehensive effort to promote academic integrity must not only focus on changing students, it must also include more systemic, cultural change at the school level. As depicted in figure 3.1, the AwI model for school change contains four dimensions that, when operating together, create a culture where "achieving with integrity" can become normative.

At the top of the model, and infusing all other components, are the core values of respect, trust, honesty, responsibility, effort, and learning. These values should serve as guideposts for all community members—students and adults—with respect to how they conduct themselves inside the classroom and beyond. Moving counter-clockwise, the next component of the model is

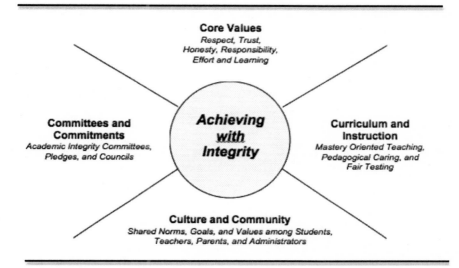

Core Values
*Respect, Trust,
Honesty, Responsibility,
Effort and Learning*

**Committees and
Commitments**
*Academic Integrity Committees,
Pledges, and Councils*

*Achieving
with
Integrity*

**Curriculum and
Instruction**
*Mastery Oriented Teaching,
Pedagogical Caring, and
Fair Testing*

Culture and Community
*Shared Norms, Goals, and Values among Students,
Teachers, Parents, and Administrators*

Figure 3.1.   The Awl Project's conceptual model for school change (Wangaard and Stephens, 2011).

"Committees and Commitments." This includes, but is not limited to, the creation of an Academic Integrity Committee that serves as an oversight and catalyzing body. A published toolkit (Wangaard and Stephens, 2011) offers detailed suggestions for creating such committees, and the kind of commitments (e.g., honor codes) that they might help to create.

The third component of this model, "Culture and Community," emphasizes the importance of developing strategies to engage and sustain the support of all constituents and stakeholders. The toolkit offers a range of suggestions for doing so, including student-led projects and initiatives that promote a culture of integrity as well as ways in which parents and other school partners might be helpful. Examples of student-led projects include an integrity pledge drive; t-shirt, poster, essay, and PSA contests; and facilitation of an "ethics café."

Perhaps the most successful of these student-led projects were the academic integrity pledge drives. At one school, the drive was undertaken by student members of the AIC in order to promote the new integrity pledge the committee had developed. To spread word of new, concise pledge, the AIC purchased business cards with the pledge printed on them as well as wristbands in school colors imprinted with *Integrity*. The AIC then set up a pledge booth at school events where they encouraged peers to sign the pledge. Those that did so received a card and wristband.

The fourth and final component of this model, "Curriculum and Instruction," focuses more squarely on what is taught and how it is taught. Again, the toolkit offers a variety of recommendations and strategies for teachers such as integrating the theme of integrity into their class expectations, syllabi, discussions, and procedures. Stephens and Wangaard (2013) acknowledged that this component was not sufficiently developed in their school-wide program. Seeing the need to do more to support teachers in promoting academic integrity within their classroom, they produced the second program of the AwI Project.

Classroom Approach: The Achieving with Integrity Seminar for Students

The AwI Seminar was designed to extend and complement the school-wide program approach. However, it can and is currently being implemented and evaluated as a stand-alone program using the format discussed below, and is suitable for implementation in high school grades.

Theoretically, the AwI Seminar is rooted in the work of James Rest and his colleagues (Rest, 1986; Rest, Narvaez, Bebeau, and Thoma, 1999) who described moral or ethical functioning as the integrated use of at least four processes: (1) *awareness* to perceive the moral dimensions of a given situation and the ability to anticipate and interpret how others might be feeling or react in that situation; (2) *judgment* to support the capacity to reason morally and render judgments about which course of action would be morally right or best; (3) commitment to increase the desire and will to act on one's moral judgments; and (4) action or the living out (through word and behavior) one's moral judgments and commitments.

Specifically, the AwI Seminar uses this four component model of ethical functioning as the basis for engaging students in a series of four discussions related to ethical dilemmas (hypothetical or real) involving academic integrity; or for use in analysis of academic content containing ethical situations. As detailed in table 3.1, each discussion is guided by a pair of core questions, a primary goal, and set of key process steps. For a more detailed description of these aspects of the AwI Seminar, see Stephens and Wangaard (in press).

Implementation Structures

The two programs of the AwI Project have different implementation structures. There is no formal professional development or training program associated with the school-wide program. Schools leaders interested in "creating a culture of integrity" need only purchase the aforementioned toolkit to get started. As detailed in the toolkit, the AwI Project prescribes the implementation of four steps or processes:

Table 3.1.   The AwI Seminar: Core questions, primary goals, and key process steps by component of ethical functioning.

	Awareness	Component of Ethical Functioning		
		Judgment	Commitment	Action
Core Questions	What's moral? Is this a moral situation?	What's right? What should *one* do?	Am I responsible? What must *I* do?	How do I do it? What skills and will are needed?
Primary Goal	Enhance students' ability to notice the moral dimensions of a given situation	Increase students' use of principled reasoning in making moral judgments	Foster students' commitment to do the "right" thing	Develop students' "will and skill" related to academic integrity
Key Process Steps	Notice, Analyze, Identify	List, Decide, Explain	Decide, Check, Confirm	Employ, Deploy, Exercise

1. *Form*—the formation of an academic integrity committee, with representatives from the student body, faculty, and administration;
2. *Assess*—conduct a school climate survey to assess teachers' and students' perceptions, beliefs, and behaviors related to academic integrity;
3. *Develop*—using data from the climate survey develop a strategic plan (goals, policies, procedures, etc.) that supports the changes desired;
4. *Implement*—implement the strategic plan developed, ensuring a consensus sense of shared responsibility among all constituents.

Of course, short of revolution, cultural change is neither easy nor quick. It is very likely the strategic plan (or some aspect of it) will require revision. Thus, it is recommended that steps 2, 3, and 4 be repeated as needed.

In contrast to the school-wide program, the implementation of the AwI Seminar for students adheres to a more finite timeline. Specifically, it is compromised of five thirty- to fifty-minute lessons (depending on the integration of content from academic curricula): one each for the four components detailed in table 3.1 plus a final synthesis lesson. Thus, the total time required to implement the AwI Seminar is relatively brief (two-and-a-half hours) and flexible (the introductory lessons can be taught over a single week or several). These characteristics make the program a highly desirable one for educators wary of making any additions to an already crowded curriculum.

In fact, the AwI Seminar was designed to be "integrated with"—not merely "added to"—existing curricula. That is, the core questions and key process steps are meant to be woven into subject area content (preferably repeatedly throughout the school year) in a way that deepens not only students' awareness, judgment, and commitment to academic integrity but also their analysis and critical thinking of subject area topics with ethical content. In this regard, the AwI Seminar is consistent with the objectives of the U.S. Common Core Standards related to developing students' higher-order thinking skills.

For example, a science teacher may begin the academic year by engaging students in an AwI discussion about the importance and meaning of integrity in scientific research. She may reference the three obligations of "responsible conduct in research" described by National Academy of Science (2009), and she may use real-world cases involving scientific fraud or controversies (such as cloning human embryos) to anchor a discussion using the AwI Seminar's core questions.

Finally, and also in contrast to the school-wide program, the AwI Seminar requires some professional development (PD) for implementation. Specifically, the authors are currently conducting a fidelity of implementation study of a web-based PD program for secondary teachers interested in using the AwI Seminar in their classrooms. The PD program consists of a series of six webinars; each requires about forty-five minutes online and the same amount of time offline "homework." Thus, the total time required is approximately ten hours.

Evidence of Effectiveness

As described in Stephens and Wangaard (2013), results from a study of the implementation of the AwI Project's school-wide program were decidedly mixed. The strategic process steps involved in the program were very effective in drawing constituents together and two of three schools successfully developed and implemented programs aimed at promoting integrity.

However, while those programs were meritorious, they did not appear to produce any significant changes in students' beliefs and behaviors related to academic integrity. The latter does not mean the program is ineffectual, but it does highlight the challenge of changing school culture and student behavior, particularly in a short period of time (i.e., less than two years).

With respect to the AwI Seminar, preliminary results indicate that among teachers who completed the online PD program and implemented the AwI Seminar in their classrooms, adherence to the use of the program's core questions and activity protocols was very high (approximately 83 percent). Quality of delivery—another important dimension of implementation fidelity—was also strong but somewhat less impressive: approximately 67 percent of the teachers demonstrated high levels of quality, and the remaining teachers medium levels. A study of AwI Seminar's effect on students' ethical functioning is scheduled for the 2014–2015 academic year.

Availability and Cost

Description of the school-wide approach is presently available in the form of a published toolkit (referenced earlier) and can be purchased from the publisher as well as from the School for Ethical for Education (SEE) for approximately $30. The toolkit outlines a multistep approach to creating a culture of academic integrity, providing not only the information needed but also pointing to the resources to do so. As noted above, the program involves creating a committee of a dozen or more school constituents. For those who would like additional support implementing the program, SEE offers a range of services: from complimentary planning services to fee-based support services.

Specifically, fees for those interested in conducting a school-wide baseline assessment on students' perceptions, beliefs, and behaviors related to academic integrity will cost $450 for the evaluation process that includes survey design, data collection and analyses, and final report. Onsite consulting services and professional development costs approximately $900 (plus travel) for a full day. Teachers and administrators interested in the AwI Seminar can enroll in the online teacher professional development program for a fee of $500 per teacher, or a reduced rate of $1,500 for a school-based team of five teachers. For more details about SEE's programs and services, please visit: http://ethicsed.org/academic-integrity.

Promise and Cautions

The two programs of the AwI Project offer a lot of hope and help to those interested in addressing the epidemic of cheating, and do so through positive developmental approaches. However, as detailed in the foregoing, a recent study of the school-wide approach produced mixed results and the effectiveness of AwI Seminar remains to be evaluated. Thus, despite offering great promise, the AwI Project is still evolving and should be adopted with mindfulness of the challenges inherent in any effort to change school culture and student behavior.

One of the most difficult challenges to promoting academic integrity in high school is the fact that it is often ignored when it comes to consistent advocacy and school policy. Like all reform efforts aimed at taking on important educational challenges, the AwI Project requires strong administrative leadership and support to take root and be successful. Similarly, high levels of teacher commitment and motivation are needed to integrate the AwI Seminar effectively into classrooms.

In sum, for those willing to make the investment needed, the AwI Project offers a promising pair of programs to promote academic integrity in high schools. The programs are well-grounded in both theory and research, and offer schools and teachers positive approaches to reducing academic dishonesty—by increasing or strengthening students' ethical awareness, judgment, commitment, and action related to academic integrity. In addition, the AwI Seminar helps students hone the skills needed to reason, analyze, and evaluate (goals of the U.S. Common Core) with a focus on the ethical acts of characters in literature, history, and science.

RESTORATIVE JUSTICE AND RESTORATIVE PRACTICES

Philip M. Brown and John Bailie

To accomplish everything a school needs—mainly academic goals—becoming a school with a restorative climate and culture is essential. My students are now in better shape—both academically and behaviorally—than they've ever been. If you're serious about becoming a restorative school, the best way to get there is with the Whole-School Change Program.
   —Rhonda Richetta, principal, City Springs Elementary/Middle School,
        Baltimore (International Institute for Restorative Practices, 2014b)

Restorative justice (RJ) and restorative practices (RP) have shown great promise as positive alternatives to current punitive approaches to school discipline. They share some common characteristics and have been successfully used in a variety of institutional settings; however there is no one definition for either. Restorative justice has historical roots stemming from practices of indigenous populations and ancient civilizations that use victim-offender mediation, circle conferences, and community conferences, as ways of dealing with conflict within their communities.

The current Western, punitive idea of discipline is an approach that focuses primarily on social sanctions and retribution and inadequately supports pathways for positive change for the offender and progress for the community as a whole. There is also lack of evidence supporting the idea that these traditional approaches in any way make school safer or prevent future misbehavior (APA Zero Tolerance Task Force, 2008). Instead of sanctions that rely on, or result in, social exclusion of the offender, RJ and RP focuses on social inclusion, acknowledging the harm done, and strengthening relationships among all those involved so that the larger community can move forward in a positive way.

As there is no one definition of restorative justice, it is often referred to as a set of techniques or processes that most always involve both the victim(s) and offender. Depending on the institutional setting and type of processes used, other people involved are typically a combination of family members, friends, community members, and other stakeholders such as teachers, school staff, and such (if being implemented within a school setting).

In some restorative justice programs there is also a mediator (typically a volunteer with no direct relation to the parties involved), who is there to mediate the discussion with some degree of objectivity. The implementation of restorative justice practices and techniques can be adjusted and implemented differently depending on the context, population, audience, and intended outcomes. Dr. Howard Zehr (2002), who is often referred to as the pioneer of the modern concept of RJ, defines it as, "a process to involve, to the extent possible, those who have a stake in a specific offense and to collectively identify and address harms, needs, and obligations, in order to heal and put things as right as possible" (37).

The primary canons of RP are intended to promote support and connection, uphold structure and accountability, and integrate fair process and student voice (Gregory, Clawson, Davis, and Gerewitz, in press, 3). RP is notably a more developmentally appropriate approach to discipline compared to more traditional and commonly used techniques such as "zero-tolerance" policies and suspensions. The sense of autonomy provided with the RP approach may be especially developmentally appropriate for high school students in contrast with using suspension from school as a reactionary disciplinary technique, or providing rewards for positive behavior with tangible reinforcements which may be more developmentally appropriate for elementary age students (Allen and Antonishak, 2008).

Implementation Model: The Whole-School Change Program

Restorative practice builds relationships. Teachers are taking charge of discipline in the classroom. There has been a decrease in students sent to the principal's office from 100 a month to two or three a month since implementing restorative practices. The most effective thing about the Whole-School Change program is that each and every person in the school has bought in. They all think about: "What are you doing for the whole school?" It's a beautiful thing.
    —Sadie Silver, principal, Warren Prep Elementary School, Brooklyn, NY
    (International Institute for Restorative Practices, 2014b)

The International Institute of Restorative Practices (IIRP) is a graduate school and professional development hub whose overall mission is to advance the education of professionals as well as to conduct research and expand the field of restorative practices. The underlying goal is to influence human behavior in a positive way and strengthen our global civil society.

IIRP has created multiple professional development projects intended to provide tools and professional training to promote restorative practices in helping solve complex social issues. The Whole-School Change program approach incorporating restorative practices was created as part of a broader SaferSanerSchools project to promote and foster relationship building between and among students and staff members of schools as well as holding students accountable for each other.

The ultimate goal of the program is to create a more positive school climate, as well as to reduce crime, violence, suspensions, expulsions, and other incidents or characteristics of a school that can be seen as negatively impacting instruction time, student learning, and progress. The program focuses not only repairing relationships and harm done, but on building relationships, with the intention of increasing students' investment in their school community.

The initial implementation of this program spans two years. It begins with intensive training by IIRP for school faculty and staff who interact directly with students. The training involves on-site workshops and consultations, development of professional learning groups, and data-based feedback for faculty and staff involved. A professional learning group (PLG) is a group of school staff and faculty members who continually collaborate in a learning-oriented manner in order to share, critically analyze, and problem solve regarding any issues that may arise regarding the implementation of practice from previous trainings and workshops by IIRP. The creation of PLGs are intended to ensure the sustainability of the RP program, transcending the exit of the IIRP staff's presence both during and after the initial two years of RP implementation process.

Program Elements

There are eleven essential elements used to make this program effective, seven of which are "school-wide." The school-wide elements refer to strategies for which all school staff that interact with the students are responsible. Three "broad-based," elements refer to strategies used by all professional staff (administrators, teachers, counselors, and social workers). The "targeted" element is a specific strategy for individuals who are expected to plan and carry out restorative conferences.

RP's Eleven Essential Elements:

1. *Affective Statements (School-wide)* are central to formal restorative practices while also being the most informal response on the RP continuum. They are used to express feelings toward both negative and positive behaviors with the ultimate goal of humanizing those involved and building a stronger relationship.
2. *Restorative Questions (School-wide)* are used strictly to address negative behavior and conflict in a nonjudgmental way, with intention to

challenge the wrongdoer in understanding how their actions impacted those harmed, for him or her to take responsibility for their negative behavior, and to give a voice to those harmed as to how things can be made right among all involved to move forward in a positive way.

3. *Small Impromptu Conferences (School-wide)* are to be used consistently in response to low-level conflict instances as a way to model a healthy conflict resolution structure through the use of restorative questions asked to both the wrongdoer(s) and those harmed.

4. *Proactive Circles (Broad-based)* are used with any group of students on a regular basis as a way for them to share ideas and to build skills in facilitation of these circles. They are not used strictly for conflict resolution or in response to particular behavior but instead are there to provide a social capital foundation for Responsive Circles. They are used to discuss things such as classroom and behavioral expectations and norms, academic goal setting, to monitor and discuss understanding of academic content, and for students to share their feelings, ideas, and experiences. With this type of circle, the hope is that students build trust and shared values among each other. Proactive circles physically consist of students and school faculty sitting in a circle without barriers, and often include a talking piece that is passed around sequentially.

5. *Responsive Circles (Broad-based)* are physically and structurally similar to Proactive Circles, however are expected to be used far less. The intended use for these circles is when there is a conflict or tensions among a group of students or an entire class. Like Small Impromptu Conferences, the intention is to address harm done, how it has affected those involved, how to solve the conflict, restore relationships, and plan for the future so it does not occur again. With these circles there is a facilitator present who sets a positive tone and models desired behavior and responses; however it is also intended to be a vehicle for positive behavior through peer pressure.

6. *Restorative Conferences (Targeted)* are a structured way to respond to serious incidents or patterns of less serious incidents that include those involved in the conflict or incident as well as their family and selected friends. The focus is on repairing harm and not making the wrongdoer feel judged or guilty, but rather to aid in the development of empathy through understanding the experience of others. These conferences include a trained facilitator who follows a strategic script that touches on giving both victim and offender a chance to share their feelings about the incident as well as the supporters (family and friends) from both the victim and offender. Restorative Questions are posed throughout the conference and the goal is to emphasize social inclu-

sion of the offender in a way that holds him or her accountable for negative actions.

7. *Fair Process (School-wide)* is a decision-making approach that emphasizes transparency and open lines of communication, where all those involved are treated with respect and fairness. In using this approach, higher levels of cooperation and understanding of the decision made regardless of who may win or lose, are expected. Fair Process is essential to the process of organizational and behavioral change and can be used with students, staff, and parents as appropriate.

8. *Reintegrative Management of Shame (School-wide)* does not try to avoid or suppress feelings of natural shame, but instead is used to anticipate the occurrence of shame when both confronting negative behavior and when positive affect is interrupted. This element is informed by *psychology of affect* and the *compass of shame* theories and not only acknowledges shame as being a regulator of social behavior but is intended to help transform and move beyond shame in a positive manner.

9. *Restorative Staff Community (School-wide)* is an element that sets the expectation for the staff community to consistently model and use restorative practices among each other to support and maintain their own healthy relationships. This is done through the use of Restorative Circles, Proactive Circles, and Responsive Circles as appropriate to solve conflicts and strengthen relationships among staff members.

10. *Restorative Approach with Families (Broad-based)* is intended to establish a genuine engagement with family members of students by valuing the knowledge and contribution of family members to the school community. This element emphasizes the idea that all interactions with family members are opportunities to build and strengthen relationships, as well as a way to consistently use restorative practices.

11. *Fundamental Hypothesis Understandings (School-wide)* is the cornerstone element that states, "human beings are the happiest, healthiest and most likely to make positive changes in their behavior when those in authority do things *with* them rather than *to* them or *for* them" (International Institute for Restorative Practices, 2014b, PDF, 19). It sets a framework to analyze daily actions with the intention of consistent intentionality of restorative practices.

Evidence of Effectiveness

When we were using a traditional punitive discipline approach, certain kids were spending more time out of school than in, and student achievement was very low. With restorative practices, discipline referrals have been cut in half;

suspensions, expulsions, and office referrals all are much improved and the amount of recurring offenders and fights has been greatly reduced. The processes are so powerful in helping kids reflect on their decisions and behavior and how they affect others.
—Sharalene Charns, director of Federal Programs, K–12 Instruction and Bilingual Education, Hamtramck, MI, School District (International Institute for Restorative Practices, 2014b)

Research History and Anticipated Outcomes

There has been much research documenting the successes of restorative practices as they have been implemented in schools, prisons, and community-based organizations as a positive alternative to traditional punitive processes for discipline. However, there still is a need for more systematic development of RP so it can be tested as an empirically based treatment. That said, single case studies of high schools have demonstrated some potential for RP's effectiveness.

There are data from RP program implementation in multiple high schools across the United States. For example, school record data from three high schools implementing the Whole-School Change program have reported positive findings (International Institute for Restorative Practices, 2014a). In one largely African American high school, violent acts and serious incidents were reduced by 52 percent compared to the previous year. In a large suburban high school there was a 70 percent drop in the number of "classroom disruption" and "disrespect to teacher" incidents reported. In a rural high school suspensions were reduced by 50 percent.

Most recent data from IIRP (September 2014), reports examples of effectiveness after the RP program was implemented in select schools. At City Springs School (K–8) in Baltimore, where 99 percent of the student population comes from families below the income poverty line, suspensions dropped from eighty-six in the 2008–2009 school year to just ten in the 2009–2010 school year.

At Hampstead Hill Academy (pre-K–8), also in Baltimore, the overall engagement and participation from families and community members increased (i.e., volunteers, participation in parent/teacher conferences, PTO participation). In the Hamtramck School District in Michigan, discipline referrals were cut in half across seven schools between RP implementation in 2009, to 2011.

Although it is acknowledged that there is a need to further investigate the correlation among the reduced rates described above and the implementation of IIRP's Whole-School Change program, it is promising to see such drastic reductions in such negative behavioral incidents and suspensions. Through the implementation of this program, schools report having seen increased social inclusion, calmer and quieter classrooms, and decreased rates of "misbehavior" by students (IIRP site).

Recognition by Standard Setting Organizations

In January 2014 the U.S. Department of Justice and the U.S. Department of Education issued a joint guideline for schools urging them to use forms of discipline that take a restorative approach as a way to improve school climate. RP has been noted in this guideline as being far more effective than zero-tolerance policies and more common discipline practices such as suspensions.

Several major research projects are currently underway testing the effectiveness of RP on reducing suspension rates, student misbehavior, and bullying incidents. For instance, the SaferSaner Whole-School program had been selected for study in fifteen middle and high schools as part of the Diplomas Now project, an initiative of the John Hopkins University's Center for the Social Organization of Schools that aims to build the evidence base of restorative practices as an effective alternative to zero tolerance (Atlantic Education Partners, 2014).

Training and Technical Assistance Model

The training and assisted implementation that IIRP offers through its Whole-School Change program spans two years and is inclusive of all school staff members. In the first year, initial preparation includes remote meetings and calls, customization of an online space to support staff, and online learning activity resources. The online space also includes preliminary discipline data from the implementing school collected by IIRP.

The remote preparation activities are followed by four days of on-site professional development sessions for the entire school staff. These sessions are intended to orient and include all those who will be involved in the project to familiarize them with restorative practice definitions, concepts, and skills that they will be using.

During this phase, the school staff is trained in how to use and implement restorative *circles* effectively for behavioral and academic improvement with the student population. Training on facilitation of restorative *conferences* and how to engage families in using restorative practices is also covered in this phase to ensure optimal usage of all available restorative techniques for both students and their families.

The implementation stage starts with a three-hour session that includes all staff members in addition to the four days of professional development sessions. This is when the development plan for implementation throughout the next two years begins to take shape. Professional learning groups (PLGs) are formed by the staff in order to provide an ongoing learning focused collaboration between the administration and staff regarding the implementation of the program.

The IIRP staff provides training for PLGs so the school staff can success-fully carry out the program even without IIRP's presence. After the initial implementation sessions there are follow-up activities for both the IIRP and school staff to ensure effective and successful ongoing sustainability of the program. These include monthly in-depth calls with school leaders and IIRP, on-site consultation days, and ongoing assistance with evaluation of the progress of implementation, and its potential impact on discipline data. The development instructors ensure the sustainability of the program after year two.

Fidelity, Adaptation Issues, and Caveats

There are concerns regarding maintaining fidelity of the program under im-plementation conditions that are often trying, and IIRP aims to address these by intense training and professional development for the staff and faculty members who will be part of the whole-school change and for implementing the eleven elements of the program. Specifically, they aim to promote fidel-ity by focusing on development of the PLGs, data-based feedback, and on-site consultations planned for both years of initial implementation.

During the second year of implementation there is a focus on training *development instructors*, which is a step to support the sustainability of the program. In this step, certain staff members are selected to train and provide professional development for new hires, and to essentially act as ambassa-dors and to share with them materials and resources from IIRP so that all staff members are able to function at a similar competence level.

Given the current state of research on the SaferSaner Whole-School mod-el, a few caveats should be kept in mind in considering full-scale implemen-tation of the project:

- IIRP does not yet have an intensive coaching model and implementing PLGs with fidelity will be critical to determining the degree to which they actually boost implementation quality.
- As is true for many of the approaches highlighted in this book, to be successful restorative approaches may require a philosophical switch away from a punitive approach. It is also possible that seeing positive results will influence this kind of shift. School administrators should con-sider if they are "ready" for such a shift.
- As of yet, little research has documented the qualities of administrative leadership required to create transformative change.
- As of yet, no studies have actually tracked whether IIRP efforts lead to sustained change over many years after consultants have left.

- More research is needed on other kinds of SEL changes in the classrooms: Are students more prosocial with one another? Are they taking more responsibility for problem solving? Given the promise of the RP approach, this research should be undertaken.

Cost Information

IIRP's Web site provides free supplemental information regarding its programs, webinars, and publications on its approach to restorative justice and school climate improvement. To receive information regarding pricing for this program, contact IIRP through its Web site at http://safersanerschools. org.

As of September 2014, the cost of the two-year RP program through IIRP is dependent on the school size. Information from IIRP indicates that Web site resources and program information is currently under revision, so the parameters and cost of this program will also most likely change in some way as the model is being refined and made more accessible. Based on the available information, it is estimated that the cost of implementing the IIRP version of the RP program with the necessary hands-on technical assistance requires the commitment of the equivalent of about half of one full-time employee to implement the recommended training and procedures.

THE VIRGINIA STUDENT THREAT ASSESSMENT PROGRAM

Philip M. Brown

> *Our school division has used the threat assessment guidelines for the past four years. The guidelines offer simple steps to evaluate the severity of an incident from horseplay to a very serious expression. I have noticed that my assistant principal and I have been more consistent in our decision making and recommending consequences and support for students and families since implementing the guidelines. We have also noticed greater support and confidence from parents when they realize we are using a research based model to guide in our decisions.*
> —L. Bernard Hairston, principal of Burley Middle School (Guidelines for Responding to Student Threats of Violence Threat Assessment, n.d.).

Program Description

Pertinent History

Over the past few decades, there have been rare but horrific incidents of mass school shootings in the United States. In the wake of the extensive media attention surrounding these events and concomitant national concern the Federal Bureau of Investigation, the U.S. Secret Service and the U.S. Department of Education supported research and supported the development of methods to assess threats to school safety at different levels.

One approach that has received significant implementation and positive evaluation is the Virginia Student Threat Assessment Guidelines (n.d.). The analysis process at the heart of the assessment can help identify underlying trends and behaviors students may share leading up to potential aggressive or oppositional behavior.

This program represents an approach to violence prevention that:

> emphasizes early attention to problems such as bullying, teasing, and other forms of student conflict before they escalate into violent behavior. School staff members are encouraged to adopt a flexible, problem-solving approach, as distinguished from a more punitive, zero tolerance approach to student misbehavior. As a result of this training, the model is intended to generate broader changes in the nature of staff-student interactions around disciplinary matters and to encourage a more positive school climate in which students feel treated with fairness and respect. (Threat Assessment, n.d., 1)

The program is also designed to provide students identified through the threat assessment process with mental health counseling services, including parental involvement. The Virginia Student Threat Assessment was first implemented in thirty-five schools during 2001–2002 school year and subsequently in 2,775 more schools in the states of Arizona, California, Colorado, and Virginia (Cornell, n.d).

Purpose and Scope

Threat assessment is defined as the process of evaluating the level of threat and the related circumstances surrounding an incident, uncovering facts or evidence, and identifying if the threat will be carried out. The threat assessment for students may bring early attention to bullying, teasing, and student conflict. The assessment uses flexible problem-solving approaches to deal with student conflict instead of a punitive zero-tolerance approach (Threat Assessment, n.d.).

The Virginia Student Threat Assessment is a set of guidelines designed to aid administrators, mental health staff, and law enforcement in assessing and responding to threat incidents involving students from kindergarten to twelfth grade. Those who pose a threat are usually victims of bullying, depression, and social, familial, or psychological problems. Many children fit this profile; however those that pose threats usually communicate an intention to do harm in some form (Virginia Student Threat Assessment Guidelines, n.d.).

Implementation Structure

Training and Technical Assistance Model

In order to implement the threat assessment process schools create a team led by the principal or assistant principal and typically including a school counselor, school psychologist, a resource officer, and others based on the staffing pattern of the individual school. The threat assessment team engages in a six-hour self-training session. The team leader outlines the expected responsibilities for each individual on the team. Each member practices a manualized seven-step process in assessing and identifying conflict and antisocial behavior, and how to make decisions based on the available evidence.

The manual describes the difference between transient threats, substantive, or serious substantive (Virginia Student Threat Assessment Guidelines, n.d.). The seven steps in order to assess a threat are: (1) evaluate the threat, (2) decide whether the threat is transient or substantive, (3) respond to transient threat with mild discipline such as an apologize or getting to know the other student, (4) decide whether the threat is substantive or serious substantive, (5) respond to the serious threat, (6) conduct a safety evaluation, (7) and implement safety plan (Virginia Student Threat Assessment Guidelines, n.d.).

One of the strengths of the procedures is that a transient threat may be able to be resolved quickly at step three without engaging the full team in a comprehensive threat assessment or in overreacting because of a zero-tolerance policy. If the threat is evaluated as transient, the principal may determine that a social intervention is more likely to be effective than a more punitive response. For example she might require the student to make amends by apologizing and explaining the behavior to those affected by the threat. If the behavior was sparked by an argument or conflict, the principal can choose to involve other team members in helping to address or resolve the problem before it becomes a serious violation of the school's disciplinary code and requires more significant consequences such as suspensions.

The threat assessment team is instructed not to be concerned simply with what the student said or did, but the context in which the threat was made and what the student intended by making the threat. The assessment takes account of the victim, time, place, and method of assault. In addition the threat assessment should consider if the threat was repeated over time, if the student has attempted to cause the conflict before, and if the student has a concrete plan. Evidence for a concrete plan can come in the form of a physical weapon or an audience of peers who are aware of a potential or ensuing planned physical altercation.

Requirements for Successful Start-up

Guideline documents are provided to prepare schools for implementing the program. The "step by step" approach is also given with detail on how to interview students with threat or how to interview the witness to a threat. All the materials provided include case studies, pre- and post-test training, review sheets, guidelines documents, and research data from other schools. Figure 3.2 shows the program decision-making implementation structure.

Evidence of Effectiveness

Status of Research History and Anticipated Outcomes

According to the program materials, principals, school administrators, and teachers have found the threat assessment structure and process to be valuable and important to building a positive school climate (Threat Assessment, n.d.). According to the Virginia Threat Assessment Guidelines, students in schools with the assessment report less bullying, greater willingness to seek help from others, and more positive perceptions of their school's climate.

In addition, schools using the Virginia guidelines had fewer long-term suspensions than schools using other threat assessment approaches. The improvement to these schools could not be attributed to other variables such as school size, socioeconomic status, neighborhood violence, or extent of security measures in the schools.

A school in the state of Virginia currently using the threat assessment program found that 41 percent of threats were incidents related to beating or hitting another student. The second largest categories of threats were vague and nonspecific ("I will get you"). Less than 30 percent involved threats of shooting or stabbing another student. The majority of threats, about 70 percent, can be classified as transient (threats that are said out of anger but will not be followed through). About 22 percent of threats reported on the Virginia Threat Assessment for this school were classified as substantive threats which were serious threats of a fight or assault. About 8 percent of threats were serious substantive threats to kill or severely injure another student (Cornell, Sheras, Gregory, and Fan, 2009).

A three-year study of forty public high schools in Virginia using randomized controls compared schools implementing threat assessment and those using traditional discipline procedures. The study found the total number of long-term suspensions and expulsions was significantly lower at schools using threat assessment. The schools that were not assigned to the treatment group were three times more likely to have expulsions and suspensions, and seven times more likely to have students threaten a violent act on another (Project Threat Assessment, n.d.).

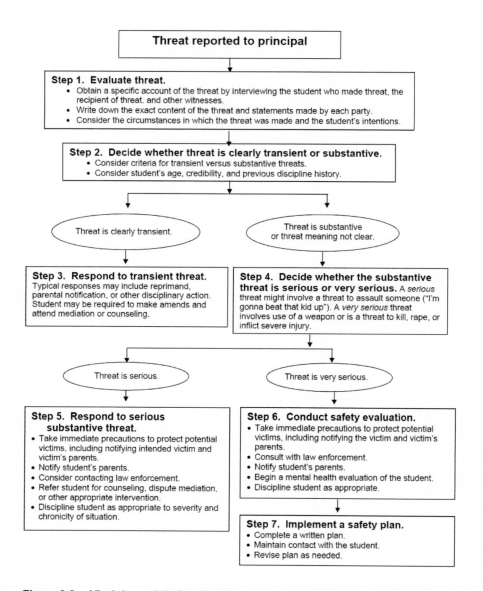

Figure 3.2.   Virginia model of student threat assessment: Implementation structure (Cornell, 2010, 5).

Caveats

The long-term impact of the threat assessment approach on school discipline is not yet clear, although it is promising. And it is not clear yet how the program impacts student prosocial behavior or if it mainly changes the procedures used by administrators and staff responsible for school safety and impacts the school climate through the alternative interventions that become part of the accepted procedures.

The materials do not address how to adapt the implementation for use with specific cultures or genders. Details on the training workshop, follow-up training, and consultation options are not described in detail. A process for monitoring fidelity of implementation to the program model is not provided, nor is a protocol for collecting and using data to track and improve target outcomes is not provided (Virginia Student Threat Assessment Guidelines, n.d.).

Availability and Cost

The guidelines can be purchased separately on Amazon for $50. A day-long site training workshop including three-hour consultation with participant evaluation is $4,000. If the school would like follow-up training, the cost will vary on length and location of site. Additional consulting via e-mail, threat documents, and training material are all free of charge.

POSITIVE BEHAVIOR INTERVENTIONS AND SUPPORTS: A MULTI-TIERED BEHAVIOR INTERVENTION FRAMEWORK

Sharon Lohrmann

Program Description and Evidence of Effectiveness

Positive Behavior Interventions and Supports (PBIS) is a multi-tiered behavior intervention framework that provides school personnel with a systematic approach to organizing their practices and interventions to address the range of student needs in a school setting (Sugai et al., 2010). The PBIS framework emphasizes a continuum of practices across three intervention tiers: Universal, Secondary, and Tertiary (Walker et al., 1996).

Derived from a public health model of intervention, the PBIS framework operates on the basis that there is a predictable pattern of response to intervention within a given population. The PBIS framework anticipates the range of intervention needs within a school setting and uses the tiered framework to implement a continuum of intervention practices.

Universal Intervention Tier

Universal interventions provide the foundation to positive and respectful learning environments by establishing a core of proactive practices applied universally across all students, staff, and settings in the school. The Universal intervention tier is, first and foremost, a systems level intervention. The objective is to promote consistency and fluency in use of practices across all staff as they interact with students.

Thus, implementation of the Universal intervention tier is designed to prepare staff with the skills, competencies, and practices to (a) use consistent and constructive language to convey conduct and climate expectations; (b) use instructional practices and activities to teach students how to meet the conduct and climate expectations; (c) provide students with frequent praise for meeting the conduct and climate expectations; and (d) use a variety of data and reflection practices to evaluate student response patterns.

Published research on the Universal intervention tier demonstrates a range of implementation outcomes including (a) decreases in office discipline referrals and suspensions; (b) academic achievement and availability of instructional time; (c) improvement in school climate; and (d) teacher well-being (e.g., Algozzine and Algozzine, 2007; Bradshaw, Mitchell, and Leaf, 2010; Horner et al., 2009; Lassen, Steele, and Sailor, 2006; Luiselli, Putnam, Handler, and Feinberg, 2005; Nelson, 1996; Ross, Romer, and Horner, 2012; Scott and Barrett, 2004). In addition to findings from research studies, state-level training initiatives have published program evaluation outcome data that includes reductions in office disciplinary patterns and academic achievement (e.g., Barrett, Bradshaw, and Lewis-Palmer, 2008; Muscott, Mann, and LeBrun, 2008).

While the application of the Universal intervention tier is subject to the strengths and needs profile of a given school, a core set of components guide implementation, including:

- Designating of a *leadership team* that includes an administrator(s), parent(s), teacher(s), student services staff (e.g., school counselor) and support staff (e.g., security guard). The leadership team is empowered to make decisions, has planned regular meetings with sufficient time allocated and uses a meeting process (i.e., agenda, workgroups, etc.) to guide their work.
- Using *a variety of data* to guide intervention decision making. During all phases of implementation the leadership team actively collects and analyzes data to inform decision making. Office discipline referrals, suspensions, attendance, tardies, and police referrals are examples of data that already exist that can provide important information about student conduct patterns and intervention needs. Surveys of students, staff, and parents designed to capture the overall climate of the building may also provide helpful information about intervention needs and effectiveness.
- Developing *an annual implementation plan* that guides the sequence and scope of PBIS intervention activities throughout the year. Interventions are linked to a school-wide expectations framework (e.g., Be Respectful,

Be Responsible, Be Safe) that is operationally defined in actionable behaviors and that instructs students on what to do in various school settings. Key interventions that are then linked to the school-wide expectations framework will include:

- A beginning of the year instruction event to teach the expectations.
- A student and staff recognition system that provides frequent praise for meeting expectations.
- Planned instruction and activities dispersed across the school year to reinforce or reteach expectations.
- Activities and events to promote community building, celebration, and cohesion among students and staff.

- *Coordinating across various committees, initiatives, and service agencies* (e.g., law enforcement and mental health) that have direct and indirect impact on school building climate and student conduct. The leadership team maximizes available resource by having a process that coordinates and communicates across groups, committees, and initiatives. At the most basic level, maintaining a matrix of all the different committees, initiatives, and services, their purpose or goal, and a contact person will provide the leadership team with the necessary information to answer the questions: who might be doing something related to our need and how can we pull them into our work?
- Using a variety of practices that *actively engage and inform school stakeholders* on an ongoing basis about implementation and student outcomes. Throughout the school year, the leadership team employs dissemination practices that provide visibility to PBIS (e.g., sharing data, newsletter updates of recent events, etc.) and opportunities for stakeholders to give feedback and shape the decision-making process.

Secondary Tier Interventions

The Secondary intervention tier is designed to provide behavior interventions to students who are displaying emerging or repeated patterns of conduct infractions or interfering behavior. As a systems level intervention, 80 percent to 90 percent of students typically respond positively to the establishment of consistent practices and language to guide student conduct (Walker et al., 1996). Approximately 10 percent to 20 percent of students will benefit from interventions in addition to those at the Universal level. This group of students will need supplemental practices to address specific skill, social, or emotional needs that interfere with displaying positive conduct.

Because the Secondary intervention tier represents a continuum of intervention need, the intervention options will vary widely in both type and

intensity. Arriving at the appropriate intervention requires a systematic process for gathering and interpreting student specific information. Secondary
tier interventions may occur in small groups (e.g., social skill instruction),
embedded into the general education routine (e.g., Check-in Check-out systems), or occur on a one-to-one basis.

The organizing structure for how Secondary tier interventions are designed and delivered will vary depending on a variety of school factors
including, the extent of the individual student's need, personnel, school size,
and school population need. Secondary tier interventions may be designed by
the classroom teacher, a grade-level teaching team, or may be the result of a
pre-referral intervention process. It is often helpful for an individual school
to have an articulated process (e.g., flowchart or sequence of steps) that
shapes the sequence of practices and decision making to determine what
level of need the student has. For example, consider how answers to the
following questions would influence the design of an articulated process at a
given school:

- What class-level interventions should the teacher use to establish routines
  and expectations within the classroom for all students?
- To what extent should the teacher independently select and use interventions before requesting assistance from a Secondary intervention planning
  team (e.g., pre-referral team)?
- How does the teacher access guidance, tools, or resources to select and try
  strategies before requesting assistance from a Secondary intervention
  team?
- What knowledge, skills, and competencies do teachers and staff have to
  select and implement Secondary tier interventions?
- How many interventions and what period of time should interventions be
  tried before requesting assistance from a Secondary intervention team?
- What criteria does the teacher apply to determine when a referral to a
  Secondary intervention team is necessary?

Tertiary Tier Interventions

A small percentage of students, around 3 percent to 5 percent, will need
intensive interventions systematically applied across the school routine. Often, but not always, students in need of Tertiary tier interventions will also
have Individual Education Plans (IEPs). It is important to note though that
Tertiary tier intervention and special education classification are not synony-
mous. Tertiary interventions extend the continuum of practice to the most
comprehensive and intensive interventions available. Behavior intervention
planning at the Tertiary tier is guided by a Functional Behavior Assessment
(FBA) and will result in a Behavior Intervention Plan (BIP) that is compre-

hensive and systematically applied across the student's school routine. Tertiary and Secondary tier interventions within the PBIS framework use the principles of behavioral science to guide the collection and interpretation of data. These principles assert that all behavior has a function and operates in a predictable pattern. When information gathering and interpretation are organized in alignment with these principles, it is possible to observe the predictable pattern and select interventions that are matched to the function of the student's behavior.

More than twenty years of research on function-based intervention planning suggests that having a systematic information gathering process grounded in the principles of behavioral science results in effective interventions and durable outcomes (e.g., Bambara, Nonnemacher, and Kern, 2009; Crone, Hawken, and Bergstrom, 2007; Dutton-Tillery, Varjas, Meyers, and Smith-Collins, 2010; Ingram, Lewis-Palmer, and Sugai, 2005; Lane, Oakes, Menzies, Oyer, and Jenkins, 2013; McIntosh, Campbell, Carter, and Dickey, 2009; Newcomer and Lewis, 2004; Scott et al., 2005; Walker, Cheney, Stage, and Blum, 2005).

Based on this expansive body of research, key components applicable to both the Secondary and Tertiary intervention tiers will include:

- Establishment of a *screening process* to identify students that meet risk criteria.
- Designated *personnel who have the skills and competencies to facilitate* function-driven intervention planning.
- A *threshold of knowledge across all school staff* about the basic principles of behavioral science (e.g., the Antecedent-Behavior-Consequence paradigm, behavior shaping and reinforcement, function of behavior, etc.).
- The use of tools and practices consistent with the principles of behavioral science and that result the identification of the variables contributing to the behavior pattern.
- A process for interpreting the data and information collected to *(a) define the function of behavior and (b) select function-based interventions*.
- The establishment of a *range of intervention options that reflect a predictable pattern of need* within the school (e.g., Check-in Check-out systems).
- A *data driven process for evaluating outcomes* for individual students and for the Secondary and Tertiary intervention tier processes.

Technical Assistance and Resources

Since 1997, The U.S. Department of Education, Office of Special Education Programs (OSEP) has funded a national Technical Assistance Center on PBIS, Co-Directed by Drs. Rob Horner, George Sugai, and Tim Lewis. In addition to influencing policy, research, and practice, the OSEP TA Center has resulted in two tangible outcomes for schools: First, the OSEP TA Center has supported the development of state-based networks that provide training and technical assistance to schools and districts interested in PBIS implementation.

Often, the state networks are funded through the state's Department of Education or collaboration of state agencies to make available training and technical assistance at no or limited cost to schools (e.g., http://www.njpbs.org, http://flpbs.fmhi.usf.edu/, http://www.pbisillinois.org/, http://www.nhcebis.seresc.net/). Interested personnel should visit http://www.pbis.org/pbis-network to locate their state coordinator on PBIS.

Second, as result of this extensive network www.pbis.org hosts a rich array of tools, resources, presentations, and information provided by Center Partners and state networks across the United States. Through the OSEP TA Center and the state network Web sites, it is possible for school personnel to find everything they need to self-guide their implementation of PBIS. One significant resource developed through the OSEP Technical Assistance Center on PBIS is the Blueprint on PBIS implementation, available at http://www.pbis.org/blueprint (Sugai et al., 2010).

The Implementation Blueprint provides a comprehensive and detailed description of the components, characteristics, and practices of PBIS implementation and serves as the premiere implementation guidance document. School personnel interested in learning more about PBIS will find the blueprint an excellent starting resource.

Caveats: Implementation Fidelity

Like all interventions, achieving positive student outcomes is dependent upon the extent to which the framework and accompanying practices are implemented with fidelity. A growing body of research findings suggests there are a number of factors that influence implementation of PBIS including administrative support, staff attitudes and beliefs, staff knowledge about PBIS components, and the availability of resources and professional development support (e.g., Coffey and Horner, 2012; Kincaid, Childs, Blasé, and Wallace, 2007; Lohrmann, Forman, Martin, and Palmieri, 2008; Lohrmann, Martin, and Patil, 2013).

Since each intervention tier has its own combination of components and practices, it is necessary to consider evaluation of fidelity for each tier separately. Evaluation of fidelity should occur at multiple points in the school year (at least fall and spring) and use multiple measures including (a) a review of student outcome data (e.g., office conduct referrals and suspensions), (b) tools designed specifically to assess implementation fidelity of PBIS, and (c) stakeholder input (e.g., climate surveys or focus groups).

School personnel should expect that achieving implementation fidelity may take two to five years of consistently employing a cycle of formative evaluation and practice improvement. A number of tools are available at www.pbis.org, free of charge, to assist school personnel to evaluate implementation fidelity including:

- *Benchmarks of Quality* (BoQ) (Kincaid, Childs, and George, 2010).
- *Schoolwide Evaluation Tool* (SET) (Sugai, Lewis-Palmer, Todd, and Horner, 2001).
- *Team Implementation Checklist* (TIC) (Sugai, Horner, Lewis-Palmer, and Rossetto-Dickey, 2012).
- *School-wide Universal Behavior Support Sustainability Index: School Teams* (SUBSIST) (McIntosh, Doolittle, Vincent, Horner, and Ervin, 2009).
- *Implementation Phases Inventory* (Bradshaw, Debnam, Koth, and Leaf, 2009).
- *Individual Student Systems Evaluation Tool* (ISSET) (Anderson, Lewis-Palmer, Todd, Horner, Sugai, and Sampson, 2012).
- *Benchmarks for Advanced Tiers* (BAT) (Anderson et al., 2011).

SUMMING UP

Systemic approaches to prosocial school discipline feature at least three features in common. First, they must address issues from a whole-school perspective; they are not just concerned with one group of students, or addressing a specific identified discipline issue. Second, they involve all staff in playing some role in the procedures or program processes that are at the heart of the preventive strategies. Third, they must see the school as a structural unit and include significant involvement by school administrators.

The four approaches described in this chapter address discipline itself from very different perspectives. Academic integrity, particularly at the high school level, is an underrepresented concern that is at the heart of the intersection between intellectual and moral growth. Restorative justice illuminates a set of practices that educators desperate for alternatives to traditional approaches need in moving from a punitive to growth oriented models of discipline.

The Virginia Threat Assessment Program sounds like it is only designed for the most potentially violent students. But, in fact, it emphasizes a flexible, problem-solving approach to all student misbehavior. It also helps initiate broader changes in staff-student interactions with the goal of providing a more positive school climate in which students feel treated with fairness and respect

Finally, the PBIS program as presented here is also designed to involved staff in an intensive and on-going process of examining meaningful data about student behavior in a way that can lead to systemic change. As can be seen from some of the school profiles in chapter 7, PBIS is not be a sufficient approach to changing school climate by itself, but can be an effective component when combined with other prevention efforts.

Chapter Four

Curriculum and Instructional Approaches

THE SECOND STEP PROGRAM

Philip M. Brown with Second Step Staff

We have all fifty-five classrooms teaching the Second Step lessons. They're all involved in it, and the principal, the other AP, and I are just as involved, too. As we walk around and see what they're doing in the school, we're amazed. We can see it. Every teacher says "Something's different this year." There is less tardiness, there's less fighting. There's less everything.
—Matthew Nelson, assistant principal, O. Henry Middle School,
Austin, Texas

History of the *Second Step Program*

The origins of the *Second Step Program* began on the streets of Seattle, Washington, when Dr. Jennifer James discovered that many homeless youth had been sexually abused. She founded a group to focus on child sexual abuse prevention, and in 1981 the group's first step was the creation of a sexual abuse prevention curriculum for children: the *Talking about Touching* program (TAT).

The group, calling itself Committee for Children, took a second step in 1986 and published the *Second Step Program* for grades 1 through 5. It was designed as a violence prevention program teaching empathy, impulse control, problem solving, and anger management. Although predating the term, the *Second Step Program* essentially was and continues to be a social-emotional learning program.

Over the next twenty-five years, the *Second Step Program* went through several editions and expanded to include preschool/kindergarten and middle school grade levels. In 2011, the fourth edition of the K–5 program and the first edition of the Early Learning Program were published. In 2014/2015, a K–5 Bullying Prevention unit and an Early Learning to Grade 5 Child Protection Unit were added.

According to a multiyear business analysis, some form of the *Second Step Program* is used in approximately 40 percent of U.S. schools. It has been translated into eleven different languages, adapted for use in Australia, and has a presence in sixty other countries.

Purpose and Scope

The *Second Step Program* is a universal, classroom-based prevention program for children from preschool through middle school. The program targets key risk and protective factors linked to a range of problem behaviors. It is designed to enhance social-emotional development through increasing empathy, self-regulation, emotion management skills, and problem-solving skills. The middle school curricula include additional content designed to prevent bullying and substance abuse.

The program is based on scripted lessons for classroom delivery by teachers or school counselors. The curricula range in length from twenty-seven weeks in Early Learning to thirteen weeks in middle school. Lessons also vary in length by age, from five to seven minutes (daily) in Early Learning to fifty to sixty minutes for middle school grades. Delivering the program involves teaching weekly lessons, supporting generalization of skills throughout the school day, and (in K–5) implementing a short Daily Practice Activity four days per week. Lessons are taught through a combination of direct instruction, stories, class-wide and small-group discussion, skill practice activities, video content, and songs. K–3 lessons contain Brain Builders that use game-like exercises to teach executive function skills.

Two additional *Second Step Program* units (Bullying Prevention Unit and Child Protection Unit) teach skills for bullying prevention and personal safety drawn from two previous evidence-based Committee for Children programs—the *Steps to Respect* program and the TAT program. The core program and both units can be taught in an entire school year. The K–5 core program and Bullying Prevention Unit lessons and family materials are available in Spanish.

Evidence of Effectiveness

A number of evaluations of the *Second Step Program*, conducted over the past several years in various grades across the United States and internationally, have examined the impact on several different student outcomes. Outlined below are the results of these studies.

Decreases in Aggression

A randomized controlled trial of the *Second Step* (3rd edition) curriculum was conducted to examine the impact of the program on aggression and positive social behavior among elementary school students ($N = 790$). Observational data indicated that physical aggression decreased among students in the *Second Step* classrooms when compared to students in the control classrooms. Six months post-program completion, students in *Second Step* classrooms continued to show lower levels of aggression. Students receiving *Second Step* lessons also showed increased prosocial behaviors at posttest when compared to children in the control classrooms (Grossman et al., 1997).

Gains in Prosocial Skills and Behavior

A pre-post design of 455 fourth- and fifth-grade students in a small urban school district was studied to evaluate the efficacy of the *Second Step* curriculum. Students who received the *Second Step Program* showed significant gains in knowledge about empathy, anger management, impulse control, and bully-proofing. Report card data also revealed modest gains in prosocial behavior (Edwards, Hunt, Meyers, Grogg, and Jarrett, 2005).

A separate study conducted with 149 African American students in fifth through eighth grade found similar results as the previous study. Using the same pre-post design, the findings revealed significant increases in self-reported knowledge and skills related to violence, self-reported empathy, and teacher-reported prosocial behavior after the students received the *Second Step Program* (McMahon and Washburn, 2003).

Decrease in Likelihood of Physical Aggression

Thirty-six middle schools in the Chicago and Wichita areas participated in an evaluation of the *Second Step* middle school program. Schools in the study were randomly assigned to either teach the *Second Step Program* or be control schools. After one year, sixth-graders in schools that implemented the *Second Step Program* were 42 percent less likely to say they were involved in physical aggression compared to sixth-graders in schools that did not implement the program (Espelage, Low, Polanin, and Brown, 2013).

International Evaluations

An evaluation of *Steg to Steg* (the Norwegian version of *Second Step*) was conducted in fifth- to seventh-grade classrooms in Norway using a quasi-experimental design. Results showed that the program resulted in significant increases in social competence for both boys and girls across the fifth and sixth grades, the two years examined in the study. In addition, boys in sixth grade who had received the program reported lower levels of externalizing problem behavior compared to control students (Holsen, Smith, and Frey, 2008).

An experimental study of the *Faustlos* program (German translation of the *Second Step Program*) was conducted with 716 children ages five to eight. Empathy and aggression were assessed by teachers and parents who completed a measure of internalizing and externalizing behaviors. After one semester, students who participated in the *Faustlos* program showed significant declines in anxious, depressed, and socially withdrawn behavior compared to the control groups, based on parents' ratings (Schick and Cierpka, 2005).

Recognition

The *Second Step Program* is included on several lists of evidence-based practice, such as the Substance Abuse and Mental Health Services Administration's National Registry of Evidence-based Programs and Practices; the Collaborative for Academic, Social, and Emotional Learning's Safe and Sound Guide; the Office of Juvenile Justice Delinquency and Prevention's Model Program Guide; and the Promising Practices Network.

Fidelity and Adaptation Issues

The *Second Step Program* has been found to be effective in geographically diverse areas, across diverse ethnic/racial and socioeconomic student groups, and has been used in the United States and Canada and adapted and translated for use in fifteen partner countries around the world. Evaluations of *Second Step*'s effects on African American and Latino children have been positive.

Implementation Structure

Training and Technical Assistance Model

The *Second Step Program* includes online training for educators implementing the program as well as a comprehensive set of multimedia resources to support implementation. Committee for Children's Client Support Services provides free technical support. Free webinars provide overviews of the program as well as topic-based information. Customized in-person training requirements are available at an additional cost.

The Bullying Prevention and Child Protection Units include a robust adult training, which includes three training modules: one each for school leaders, all school staff, and lesson implementers.

Requirements for Start-up

There are minimal requirements for starting the program; all online training and resources are included in the price of the curriculum.

Sustaining the Program over Time

Once the program is purchased, all lessons, online training, and resources can be used year after year. In addition, implementation resources to encourage sustainability over time are also available.

Availability, Cost, and Contact Information

Cost of the Program

The cost of the core program varies slightly by grade level with an average cost of $379 for the core program and $179 for the units (2014 prices). Discounts are available for district-wide implementation. There are no associated consumables or recurring costs. All implementation training is included in the cost of the program.

Contact Information

Web site: cfchildren.org. Phone: 1-800-634-4449. Email: info@cfchildren.org

Funding Supports

Schools and school districts have used the funds from the following sources to purchase SSP: Title I and Title II, Individuals with Disabilities Education Act (IDEA), Office of Juvenile Justice and Delinquency Prevention (OJJDP), Substance Abuse and Mental Health Services Administration (SAMSHA), 21st Century Community Learning Centers. Federal grants such as Safe Schools, Healthy Students have also been used. In addition school or district prevention, school safety, character education, discretionary or community funds have been accessed.

THE LEARNING TO BREATHE PROGRAM

Patricia Broderick

I'm usually a lot more stressed than I think I am all the time, just from school and home and everything that's going on, and I try to cover it up. But when I do this breathing, it helps me release all this stress I guess, and it's really helped me a lot.

—Middle school student (NewHarbingerPub, 2013, n.p.)

Program Description

Learning to Breathe (L2B) is a mindfulness-based curriculum that is intended to facilitate the development of attention and social and emotional skills in adolescents. L2B aims to help students understand their thoughts and feelings, learn how to manage uncomfortable emotions, learn about the nature and consequences of chronic stress, expand their repertoire of stress management skills, incorporate mindfulness into their daily life, and provide opportunities to practice these skills in a group setting.

Emotion regulation is strengthened by cultivating meta-cognitive strategies that lead to decentering from thoughts and feelings in ways that allow for simple observation and decrease experiential avoidance. Self-management is enhanced though nonjudgmental observation of experience that serves to diffuse the intensity of emotions and, potentially, the subsequent drive to act on them automatically.

Six themes are built around the BREATHE acronym:

- B (Body)—body awareness.
- R (Reflections)—understanding and working with thoughts.
- E (Emotions)—understanding and working with feelings.
- A (Attention)—integrating awareness of thoughts, feelings, and bodily sensations.
- T (Tenderness/Take it as it is)—practicing compassion.
- H (Healthy Habits of Mind)—cultivating positive emotions and integrating mindfulness into daily life. The overall goal of the program is to cultivate emotional balance and inner empowerment.
- E (Empowerment)—using the practice of mindfulness as a way of gaining the "inner edge" (table 4.1).

Implementation Structure

These themes can be taught in a variety of settings, such as classrooms, clinical settings, and after-school programs. The sequence may be taught in six sessions or expanded into twelve, eighteen, or even more sessions depending on the time available. Versions of L2B have been used successfully with groups from late elementary school through undergraduate populations.

In some places, the program is being used with older adults as well. Booster activities are included for settings such as schools to promote daily mindfulness practice and reinforce the lessons of L2B. The ultimate goal is to infuse the practice of mindfulness into the daily life of the school or institution, and L2B may be one way to introduce this practice to all students using the framework of universal prevention.

This program is informed by the seminal work of a number of researchers and clinicians. In particular, L2B adapts themes and mindfulness practices from Mindfulness-Based Stress Reduction (MBSR) developed by Kabat-Zinn (1990) into a program that is developmentally appropriate, accessible to students, and compatible with school curricula. The L2B program is linked to various state and national performance standards in areas such as health, wellness, and counseling.

In its current form, each lesson includes a short introduction of the topic, several activities for group participation and discussion to engage students in the lesson, and an opportunity for in-class mindfulness practice. Downloadable workbooks and audio files for home mindfulness practice are provided to participants as part of this program. The sequence of class sessions is expanded in table 4.1.

L2B program development was based on research-based knowledge about adolescent development (see Broderick and Blewitt, 2014). Adolescents are involved at a deep psychological level with constructing an identity and developing autonomy from adults. Emotions can become overwhelming and confusing, and although adolescents' ability to understand and manage emotions can advance, training in this area has often been neglected in school settings.

The group-based format of L2B provides support for the exploration of emotion regulation strategies and invites participants to consider the usefulness of these tools for their lives. The discussion and practice sessions complement adolescents' increased capacity for introspection while maintaining sensitivity to adolescents' internal pressure for social conformity and tendency toward social comparison. Non-intrusive discussion of general stressors facilitates self-discovery in the peer context. Finally, the active participation of students in practice, in-class, and at home supports integration of program content.

Evidence of Effectiveness

To date, two published studies, three dissertations, and two unpublished research studies (details available at http://learning2breathe.org/curriculum/research) have reported improvements in various measures as outcomes of L2B. The pilot study (Broderick and Metz, 2009) included a total class of 120 female students (mean age = 17.4) from a private school who participated as part of their health curriculum.

Table 4.1. BREATHE: The six themes.

Letter/Theme	Message of Each Theme	Contents
B (Body)	Listen: Your body is trying to tell you something.	Introduction to mindfulness and mindlessness; mindfulness in everyday activities; practice in somatic awareness.
R (Reflections/ thoughts)	Thoughts are just thoughts.	Discussion, activities, and practice designed to understand automatic self-talk and to approach it using mindfulness.
E (Emotions)	Surf the waves of your emotions.	Discussion, activities, and practice designed to understand how emotions affect thoughts and bodily sensations; practice in handling emotions mindfully.
A (Attention)	Attention to body, thoughts, and feelings is good stress management.	Discussion, activities, and practice designed to understand stress and stress reactivity.
T (Tenderness/Take it as it is)	Learn to be kind to yourself	Discussion, activities, and practice designed to cultivate kindness and self-compassion as opposed to meanness.
H (Healthy Habits of Mind)	Practice healthy mind habits to reduce stress and increases inner strength.	Wrap-up of all sessions and discussion of how to use mindfulness in one's life.
E (Empowerment)	Gain the inner edge.	Overall program goal

Relative to controls, participants reported decreased negative affect and increased feelings of calmness, relaxation, and self-acceptance. Improvements in emotion regulation and decreases in tiredness and aches and pains were significant in the treatment group at the conclusion of the program. Qualitative feedback indicated a high degree of program satisfaction. The results suggested that mindfulness was a potentially promising method for enhancing adolescents' emotion regulation and well-being.

A second study (Metz et al., 2013) included 216 regular education public high school boys and girls with pretest and posttest data participating in the program or an instruction-as-usual comparison condition in a matched school. L2B was delivered within a classroom by the classroom teacher who had received prior training. Program participants reported statistically lower levels of perceived stress and psychosomatic complaints and higher levels of efficacy in affective regulation. Program participants also evidenced statistically larger gains in emotion regulation skills including emotional awareness, access to regulation strategies, and emotional clarity. These findings provide promising evidence of the effectiveness of L2B when taught by school staff on the development of key social-emotional learning skills.

Availability

The L2B curriculum, which includes in-depth descriptions of group activities, practice scripts, and other teacher resources, is available from New Harbinger Publications (https://www.newharbinger.com/learning-breathe). The complete student workbooks (for both a structured six-week and extended eighteen-session version of the course) are free to download from the publisher once the purchase of the book is registered on its Web site.

The posters and audio files for four short mindfulness practices (body scan, mindfulness of thoughts, mindfulness of emotions, and loving-kindness) are also free to download. Hard copies of the workbook may be purchased from New Harbinger.

Contact Information

Workshops to train educators in both the background of mindfulness practices and implementation of L2B in schools can be arranged by contacting Dr. Trish Broderick at pcb13@psu.edu. Although L2B workshops may also be designed to provide an introduction to mindfulness for those without prior experience, it is recommended that participants who plan to use L2B in the classroom or with other educators have some prior mindfulness experience intended for adults. Additional resources on mindfulness-based approaches and training can be found at the Web sites for the following organizations:

- Center for Contemplative Mind
- Center for Investigating Healthy Minds
- Center for Mindfulness@UMASS
- Collaborative for Academic, Social, and Emotional Learning (CASEL)
- Garrison Institute
- Mind and Life Institute
- Mindfulness in Education
- Penn State Prevention Research Center
- UCSD Mindfulness Center

SUMMING UP

There are many curricular approaches and programs that rest on sound developmental principles and can have a positive impact on school climate and student behavior. The Collaborative for Academic, Social, and Emotional Learning has reviewed and rated the evidence supporting many of these, as mentioned in chapter 1.

The two programs described in this chapter represent both the largest and arguably the most completely organized and accessible program (*Second Step*), and one of the newest approaches that has shown great promise in early research in being of direct assistance to both students and teachers in learning skills to help manage their feelings and behavior (The Learning to Breathe Program).

The important note here is that the right formula for prosocial disciplinary approaches includes both structural and systemic policies and practices as well as skill-based instruction delivered in the classroom and modeled as a natural part of adult-student interactions and relationships.

Chapter Five

Programmatic Approaches

THE CARING SCHOOL COMMUNITY PROGRAM

Peter Brunn

> *After we brought Caring School Community on site I saw the children treat each other more respectfully; we weren't dealing with the fighting which took place regularly my first year here.*
> —Michael Sahlman, teacher leader, Oakland Unified School District

Program Description

Caring School Community (CSC) is a nationally recognized, research-proven program of the Center for the Collaborative Classroom that builds students' sense of community in the classroom, across grades, school-wide, and with their families. It focuses on strengthening students' "connectedness" to school, which has been shown to be pivotal in promoting academic motivation and engagement and in reducing problem behaviors such as substance abuse, violence, and those emanating from mental health issues.

The program also contains proactive approaches to discipline and classroom management called developmental discipline. CSC seeks to support students in taking responsibility for their behavior while fostering their social and moral development. The program does not rely on rewards and punishments. Instead teachers use reflection, reminders, the teaching of social skills, and restoring relationships to support students' development. There are four core principles that underlie the CSC program:

- *Respectful, supportive relationships*: Stable, supportive relationships with peers and adults create a sense of safety and belonging for students, allowing them to take the risks that deep learning entails. Mutually respectful relationships among teachers and between families and the school enable communication and coordination in the students' best interests.

- *Opportunities for collaboration*: Students learn to work with others through opportunities to collaborate in academic group work, community service, tutoring, and other activities. By doing so, they cultivate both concern for others and the motivation to work for the welfare of others.
- *Opportunities for autonomy and influence*: When students have a genuine say in the life of the classroom and school, they become committed to the decisions they have helped make and feel responsible to the community they have helped shape.
- *Emphasis on common purposes and ideals*: When a school community deliberately emphasizes the importance of learning and of behaving humanely and responsibly, students have standards of competence and character by which to live and learn.

The above principles are embodied in the four major components of the current CSC program, which are:

- *Class meetings*: This forum allows teachers and students to get to know one another, discuss issues, identify and solve problems, and make decisions that affect classroom climate, including the setting of norms—a shared teacher-student responsibility for addressing expectations and behaviors within the classroom.
- *Cross-age Buddies activities*: The Buddies program pairs whole classes of older and younger students for academic and recreational activities. These activities help build caring, cross-age relationships and create a schoolwide climate of trust.
- *Homeside activities*: Students complete these short conversational activities (included in both English and Spanish versions) at home with their parent or caregiver and then debrief back in their classroom. These activities validate the families' perspectives, cultures, and traditions and promote interpersonal understanding and appreciation.
- *School-wide community-building activities*: These innovative, inclusive, and collaborative activities link students, parents, and school staff in building a caring school environment. These activities foster new school traditions and promote involvement of parents who typically do not participate at school.

When CSC is fully implemented, the above principles and approaches inform decisions about school policy, pedagogy, structure, and content, and become embodied in the myriad choices that every member of the school staff makes every day.

Implementation Structure

Schools and districts develop implementation plans in partnership with Developmental Studies Center consultants. These plans take into consideration the school or districts needs and their internal capacity to support teachers. Typically a professional development plan is created for teachers, principals, and school leadership teams. The leadership teams consist of the principal and at least two teacher leaders. If present, this team might also include the school counselor or social worker.

All implementations involve the adoption of the Caring School Community program materials. These materials are designed for each classroom teacher. There is also an additional leader's kit that goes to the principal. Successful implementations that are sustained over time include three necessary conditions:

- Strong principal support and direct involvement with the program.
- A strong school leadership team.
- An ongoing professional development plan for teachers.

Evidence of Effectiveness

> *For our school the benefits of CSC have been students feeling they have more of a voice about what is happening in their classroom and in the school. There are structures in place for them to talk and be listened to both among their peers and teachers and the whole school.*
> —Katii Hazen, principal, Oakland Unified School District

CSC is the oldest program of the Center for the Collaborative Classroom. It has been developed, implemented, tested, and refined over a period of more than thirty years. It has proven to be highly effective in a number of rigorous evaluation studies, and the results have been published in research journals in both education and psychology. These studies of CSC have found the following outcomes:

- Greater sense of the school as a caring community.
- Stronger academic motivation.
- Less use of alcohol and marijuana.
- Better conflict resolution skills.
- Stronger commitment to democratic values.
- More concern for others.
- Safer learning communities.
- Improved student discipline.

- Improved academic achievement. (Battistich, Schaps, and Wilson, 2004; Brunn, 2014; Schaps, Battistich, and Solomon, 2004; Solomon, Battistich, Watson, Schaps, and Lewis, 2000; Watson, 2014)

CSC has been recognized by a number of organizations and clearing-houses as a model character education and social and emotional learning program. Federal, state, and other organizations include:

- U.S. Department of Education, What Works Clearninghouse http://ies.ed. gov/ncee/wwc/InterventionReport.aspx?sid=7.
- Substance Abuse and Mental Health Services Administration (SAMHSA), National Registry of Evidence-based Programs and Practices (NREPP).
- National Institute on Drug Abuse (NIDA). http://www.drugabuse.gov/ publications/preventing-drug-abuse-among-children-adolescents/chapter-4-examples-research-based-drug-abuse-prevention-progr-0.
- U.S. Department of Justice, Office of Juvenile Justice and Delinquency Prevention (OJJDP).
- California Healthy Kids Resource Center.
- CASEL Guide http://www.casel.org/guide—An Educational Leader's Guide to Evidence-based Social and Emotional Learning (SEL) Programs, created by Collaborative for Academic, Social, and Emotional Learning (CASEL), provides school leaders with a comprehensive, rigorous review of programs. The Caring School Community program was identified as a "select" program, making it one of the highest-rated programs among nearly eighty programs reviewed.
- Educational Leadership—Educational Leadership is the flagship publica-tion of the Association for Supervision and Curriculum Development (ASCD). In the March 2003 issue, the Caring School Community program was identified as an effective program in two separate articles.

Availability, Cost, and Contact Information

The Caring School Community program comes in teacher packages in grades K–6.

- Each classroom package costs $250.00.
- The Leaders Package costs $500.00.
- Professional Development costs vary depending on the level of the materi-als purchase, the amount of online support, and the number of days re-quested. Costs typically begin at $2,600.00/day (including travel ex-penses).

For more information contact the Center for the Collaborative Classroom through their Web site at https://www.collaborativeclassroom.org/caring-school-community.

THE PLAYWORKS PROGRAM

Jill Vialet

Playworks is a unique program that responds to the national decline in youth fitness and the related obesity crisis, especially in high poverty and underserved public schools. More than that, it honors research that is documenting the important contribution that free and guided play makes to the development of both social and cognitive development.

According to a recent report by the Institute of Medicine of the National Academies called *Educating the Student Body: Taking Physical Activity and Physical Education to School*, 44 percent of the nation's school administrators have cut significant amounts of time from physical education, arts, and recess so that more time could be devoted to reading and mathematics since the passage of No Child Left Behind in 2001.

The percentage of schools offering physical education daily or at least three days a week has declined dramatically from 2001 to 2006. It is also estimated that only about half of America's youth meet the current evidence-based guideline of the U.S. Health and Human Services Department of at least sixty minutes of vigorous or moderate-intensity physical activity daily (IOM, 2013).

According to Harold Kohl, chairman of the committee that developed the Institute of Medicine report, it makes sense that schools should be involved in the effort to get children to be more active. Children are in school for many hours every day, and schools are already invested in health issues such as childhood immunizations and nutrition, which they know makes a difference in attendance and learning. The payoffs are far more encompassing than just lowering the number of children with obesity. They include increasing evidence that optimal physical activity enhances academic performance and benefits mental health, and skeletal and metabolic health as well (IOM, 2013).

What is the relationship between play and learning? The National Institute for Play (NIP) has collected a significant body of research that answers this question using data from studies of both primates and humans. The conclusion: Play is a catalyst for learning at any age. The science of play is validating what gifted educators have practiced and advocated for years. When students have fun learning, they continue to pursue it for its own sake.

Nature seems to have provided play as a way to motivate us to learn about the world and our places in it.

Play helps us retain and enhance meaningful context and optimizes social learning processes. The increased emphasis on academic rigor and high-stakes testing that began with the No Child Left Behind Act has been followed by diminished recess, art, and music and curricular designs that leave students and teachers unsatisfied and not having much fun. Play can be the gateway to vitality (Brown, n.d.).

By its very nature, play is both unique and intrinsically rewarding. As Dr. Stuart Brown, the founder of the NIP, puts it, "play generates optimism, encourages us to seek out novelty, makes perseverance fun, leads to mastery, gives the immune system a bounce, fosters empathy and promotes a sense of belonging and community" (Brown, n.d.).

What are the implications of the research on play for the preventing the kind of aggressive, antisocial behavior that concerns educators responsible for student discipline? Part of the evidence that provides strong hints at the answer comes from animal studies. Brown (n.d.) found, for example, that wolves deprived of the opportunity for play become less able to deter aggression or socialize comfortably with fellow pack members. These same socialization deficits are remediated by the availability of play in developmentally appropriate forms; the mammals studied achieved more social normalcy and they returned to nonviolent playful alternative behaviors. Would we want less for our children than for our animal friends?

Program Description

Playworks is the leading nonprofit in the country leveraging play to promote healthy behaviors and increase physical activity. Through eighteen years of application and rigorous evaluation, Playworks has developed an inexpensive and replicable model that increases children's physical activity during recess, a time in the school day that has been largely overlooked as an opportunity for promoting healthy behaviors.

Playworks was founded in 1996 at two schools in California and has grown into a $35 million organization. In 2014–2015, Playworks will directly serve 190,000 students every school day at 421 low-income elementary schools in twenty-three cities across the country. Additionally, through its professional development training program, Playworks will reach an additional 250,000 children at one thousand schools and organizations throughout the United States.

With a core belief that the power of play brings out the best in every child, Playworks's mission is to improve the health and well-being of children by increasing opportunities for physical activity and safe, meaningful play. Play, a universally accessible activity, is used to establish new norms for respectful social behavior and to include every child in physical activity. At a Playworks school, every student is included regardless of athletic ability, academic skills, or economic background.

Playworks's vision is that, one day, every child in the United States will have access to safe, healthy play at school, every day. Its goal is to establish play and recess as a core strategy for improving children's health and well-being. Playworks's path to scale includes these key markers of success:

- Play is widely accepted as a strategy for improving outcomes for children.
- The education sector values social-emotional skills and physical activity as essential elements for improving children's health and ability to learn.
- School systems invest in play.
- Every child is empowered to lead with empathy and inclusion.

Evidence of Effectiveness

The Robert Wood Johnson Foundation, the nation's leading public health foundation, invested more than $32 million in Playworks during the nonprofit's major expansion phase, confident in the program's positive impact on children's health.

In 2013, Stanford University and Mathematica Policy Research released results of a rigorous, randomized controlled trial of Playworks. Two studies using findings from this work found that as a result of Playworks's programming, students were engaged in more vigorous physical activity, schools experienced less bullying incidents, and teachers reported that students felt safer.

Additionally, at Playworks partner schools, teachers had more time for teaching, and students behaved better and were more ready to learn (Beyler et al., 2013; Fortson et al., 2013). The research raises the possibility that what happens at recess can affect a school's learning environment in important ways and that improving recess may enable schools to address a number of pressing issues at the same time.

Key findings of the study include:

- *Less Bullying.* Teachers in Playworks schools reported significantly less bullying and exclusionary behavior during recess compared to teachers in control schools—a 43 percent difference in average rating scores.
- *Increased Feelings of Safety at School.* Playworks teachers' average rating of students' feelings of safety at school was 20 percent higher than the average rating reported by teachers in control schools.
- *More Vigorous Physical Activity.* Accelerometer data showed that children in Playworks schools spent significantly more time in vigorous phys-

ical activity at recess than their peers in control schools (14 percent versus
10 percent of recess time—a 43 percent difference).
* *Ready to Learn.* Teachers in Playworks schools reported spending significantly less time to transition from recess to learning activities (34 percent
fewer minutes).

Implementation Structure

Playworks's broad adoption strategy is a training program that is available
throughout the United States and internationally to any school or youth service organization interested in more effectively integrating play into their
approach. Trainings range from a one-day Power of Play workshop designed
to strengthen playground staff's proactive group management and game facilitation skills to the more comprehensive Recess 360, lasting five to eight
months, and designed to immerse a school in a more innovative approach to
leveraging recess time as a core of school climate. Playworks training can
also be customized to meet specific needs for both schools and organizations,
with ongoing consultation provided to schools and individuals who have
participated in the workshops.

Program Availability, Cost, and Contact Information

To be eligible for Playworks's full-time program, schools must serve populations where at least 50 percent of students are eligible for free or reduced
lunch. Well-trained adult "coaches" are placed at low-income partner elementary schools to teach and model new language and activities—on the
playground, in the classroom, before and after school, and at sports leagues.
Coaches impart new social, emotional, and cognitive skills that engage students in healthy and fun ways, shifting the school climate so it becomes
uncool to exclude or ridicule any child for any reason.

Unlike many school-based programs, Playworks operates in low-income
schools *every* day of the school year, and play is used to improve the educational climate for *every* student. Costs for the direct service model vary by
region. Rates are based on program length, number of participants, and travel
fees. According to the study by Fortson and colleagues (Fortson et al., 2013),
average cost for implementation of the program in the initial year is $17,861.

THE *RESPONSIVE CLASSROOM* PROGRAM

Mary Beth Forton

The Responsive Classroom approach provides prime evidence that social and emotional teaching strategies, when well-constructed, lead to improved classroom behavior and academic growth.
—Roger Weissberg, chief knowledge officer, Collaborative for Academic, Social, and Emotional Learning

Program Description

Responsive Classroom is an elementary-level, evidence-based approach to teaching. Its purpose is to ensure a high-quality education for every child, every day. The *Responsive Classroom* approach gives teachers practical techniques for engaging students academically and building an environment conducive to learning. It rests on the foundational idea that strong classroom management, high academic engagement, positive community, and developmentally responsive teaching are all interrelated and crucial to student success.

Responsive Classroom was started in 1981 by a group of public school educators who had a vision of bringing together social and academic learning throughout the school day. Since then, more than 120,000 teachers have participated in *Responsive Classroom* professional development. Today, *Responsive Classroom* practices impact an estimated 1 million students each year.

The *Responsive Classroom* approach to discipline consists of utilizing a set of highly practical, positive approaches to teaching students self-discipline. Teachers and school leaders learn how to:

- Establish clear expectations for behavior from day one of school.
- Teach students to articulate their learning goals.
- Create classroom and school rules that connect to students' goals.
- Use techniques such as Interactive Modeling to teach positive behavior.
- Use skillful teacher language to reinforce positive behavior, quickly stop misbehavior, and respectfully restore positive behavior.
- Collaboratively solve behavior problems with students and their parents.

Educators who use the *Responsive Classroom* approach often note its transformative power. Sixth-grade teachers Lindsay Shea and Tricia Incrocci explain it this way: "*Responsive Classroom* practices have transformed our classrooms, enabling us to create a culture of caring and to build strong connections with our students. . . . We could not teach effectively without *Responsive Classroom*'s guidance in social and emotional learning!"

Evidence of Effectiveness

Research has found that the *Responsive Classroom* approach is associated with greater teacher effectiveness, higher student achievement, and improved school climate.

Most notably, two University of Virginia studies (Rimm-Kaufman and Chiu, 2007; Rimm-Kaufman, Fan, Chiu, and You, 2013) found that teachers' use of *Responsive Classroom* practices is associated with:

- Improved social skills in children.
- Improved teacher-student interactions.
- Improved emotional support for students and improved classroom organization.
- More positive feelings toward school among children and teachers.
- Higher quality standards-based instruction.
- Greater math and reading achievement among students regardless of socioeconomic background.
- Greater academic gains for low-achieving students.

More information can be accessed at http://responsiveclassroom.org/research.

Based on the strength of this research, the *Responsive Classroom* approach was identified as one of only twenty-three programs included in *Effective Social and Emotional Learning Programs: Preschool and Elementary School Edition*, CASEL's (2012) 2013 guide to preschool and elementary programs that are "well-designed, evidence-based social and emotional learning programs with potential for broad dissemination to schools across the United States" (4).

The *Responsive Classroom* approach is also recognized in the Model Program Guide of the U.S. Department of Justice, Office of Juvenile Justice and Delinquency Prevention as a promising program for delinquency prevention.

Implementation Structure

Responsive Classroom offers a range of services for schools and districts, including onsite and offsite trainings, consultation, coaching, and resources for school-based study. More than thirty years of experience have shown that *Responsive Classroom* implementation works best when:

1. There is strong support from the school leader for the approach.
2. *Responsive Classroom* consultants provide professional development for all adult members of the school community.

3. The adults in the school commit to working together as a professional learning community.

The whole-school professional development model is the most efficient and cost-effective way to achieve high-quality and broad implementation of *Responsive Classroom* strategies in a school or district. The whole-school package can be offered during the school year or summer and includes the following six components:

1. *Resources for introducing the* Responsive Classroom *approach* at a staff meeting, including a DVD and conversation guide.
2. *Four-day (twenty-eight hours)* Responsive Classroom *Course (RCC)* focused on the skills and practices of building positive community, effective management, engaging academics, and developmentally responsive teaching. Participants explore key *Responsive Classroom* teaching practices: Morning Meeting, Academic Choice, Rule Creation, Interactive Modeling, Positive Teacher Language, and Responding to Misbehavior. Instructional materials for up to thirty participants are included. The course can be completed in four consecutive days or in up to three visits to a school.
3. *A one-day workshop for up to thirty staff* to either introduce the *Responsive Classroom* approach to additional staff or to deepen the practice of staff who attended the RCC. Schools can choose from one of six workshops, including a workshop designed especially for support staff or special area teachers.
4. *A series of interactive, online learning sessions for school leaders* to learn strategies for supporting *Responsive Classroom* implementation. The online learning sessions are in Blackboard Learn™ and are available on demand with an interactive discussion component.
5. *The* Responsive Classroom *Assessment Tool for Teachers* for RCC participants. This tool helps school leaders and staff monitor growth and make decisions about ongoing professional development.
6. *A rich array of* Responsive Classroom *resources,* including fifteen copies of *Yardsticks: Children in the Classroom Ages 4–14,* third edition, and the *Responsive Classroom* Resource Library, a comprehensive collection of twenty books and a set of child development pamphlets.

Individuals can also attend *Responsive Classroom* courses at advertised locations throughout the country.

Availability, Cost, and Contact Information

Consultants are available to work with schools in all fifty states, in Canada, and in English-speaking international schools. The 2014 tuition for an individual to attend a four-day training at an advertised location is $729. Onsite trainings can also be provided for a school or district. School leaders can contact the school service team at schoolservices@responsiveclassroom.org or 800-360-6332 ext. 156 to discuss the whole-school package outlined above, or district package prices, and to create a professional development plan that matches their specific needs and budget. For more information contact the Northeast Foundation for Children, Inc. / Responsive Classroom through their Web site at https://www.responsiveclassroom.org.

Cautions and Critiques

Researchers at the University of Virginia's Curry School of Education found that the level of support provided by the principal had a significant effect on teachers' implementation of the *Responsive Classroom* approach. Specifically, teachers were more likely to use these practices when their principal showed genuine buy-in to the *Responsive Classroom* approach and when their school climate offered validation and social support for trying the *Responsive Classroom* approach (Wanless, Patton, Rimm-Kaufmann, and Deutsch, 2013). To ensure high-level implementation, principals are encouraged to attend the 4-day trainings with their staff and take a hands-on approach to leading the initiative.

THE RIPPLE EFFECTS PROGRAM

Alice Ray

Program Description

Ripple Effects is a woman-owned, social enterprise founded in 1997 with a mission to use emerging technologies to reduce social injury and promote school and life success among children and youth. Through learner-centric, expert system technology, Ripple Effects provides a flexible way to scale personalized, evidence-based, on-site emotional, behavioral, and mental health support services for elementary, middle and high school students. Currently it is used in approximately four thousand schools in 650 school districts for tiered behavioral and mental health supports, affecting more than 300,000 students annually.

One of the unique features of Ripple Effects is that it provides universal, targeted, and indicated interventions addressing a broad range of children's social, emotional growth, and mental health needs. It uses a *comprehensive, technology-based* platform that facilitates adaptation both at the level of content/salience and process/learning differentiation. The system uses students' natural selection patterns to identify and serve up the most relevant set of evidence-based strategies (along with science-based information) to address the problems they are having and the skills they need, kind of like a shoe store offering a set of options based on customer's foot size and goals. Learners select the ones that are the best personal fit.

Best practices are derived from research and theory, but delivered through the voices of peers built into the Ripple Effects software. There is no adult authority figure in the youth programs. Children and adolescents get direct access to evidence-based, trauma-informed approaches to behavioral health in a variety of school contexts: discipline, counseling, special education, computer lab, alternative, and advisory settings.

There is no one-size-fits-all methodology that works with every child. That's why Ripple Effects uses a *whole spectrum* of methodologies (cognitive, behavioral, affective, social skill, social organizing) that have proven effective for children of different ages, backgrounds, and needs. Diverse instructional modalities used in the program include: mini–case study, cognitive framing, direct instruction, peer modeling, true stories, assisted journaling, transfer training, role play, assessment of content mastery (game based), and interactive self-profiles. All are offered within a motivational counseling framework that leaves power securely in the hands of the learner.

Ripple Effects is an integrated, technology-enabled system, that includes:

- *Research-based, digital assessment tools*: for groups and individuals, student self-report, teacher observation forms, and school safety profilers for students and staff.
- *More than four hundred interactive, direct-to-learner interventions* with science-based information, motivational counseling, and skill training matched to each learner.
- A *learning platform* that provides no fewer than nine multimedia modes of instruction for every interactive tutorial.
- *Automated dosage and progress tracking.*
- *Cloud-based, HIPPA certified secure record storage.*
- *Privacy-shielded, shared data reports.*

The Ripple Effects digital resource adds value to prevention and intervention programs in the following ways:

1. *Provides a flexible, common resource across settings*, with a shared data management system to facilitate greater coordination of services.

2. *Supplements, does not replace, existing counseling, social work, and teaching resources*; allows counselors to triage resources more effectively.

3. *Expands ability to provide and sustain a tiered system of interventions without investment* in separate prevention curricula. Preconfigured treatment plans and scopes and sequences for more than sixty areas are included with software purchase.

4. *Reduces burden on teachers.* Locating both content expertise and instructional methodologies "in the box" fundamentally shifts the role of adult staff from unrealistic "sage on the stage" to the more realistic, facilitative role of "guide on the side."

5. *Is automatically adaptive and personalized.* A LEGO-like system of thousands of micro, media components is logically linked through an expert system that enables literally millions of personalized intervention options to be created on the spot.

6. *Increases protections for student privacy*, thereby addressing a major psychosocial barrier to accessing live counseling.

7. *Embeds school climate coaching for teachers, counselors and social workers.*

Evidence of Effectiveness

Ripple Effects is supported by strong evidence of effectiveness for all three tiers of intervention (see figure 5.1). SAMHSA's National Registry of Evidence-based Programs and Practices (n.d.), has awarded Ripple Effects a 3.4 (out of 4) rating for quality of research. It is notable that the program received a 4.0 rating for implementation fidelity, because both content and instructional methodologies are fully contained within the software. It is also highly rated on the National Drop Out Prevention Model Program list for all three tiers of intervention, and on Juvenile Justice and Children's Health Model program registries in several states.

Summary of Significant Positive Findings (< .05) for Ripple Effects Intervention System

(For sources for the following research summaries, see under References reported studies by Bass, Perry, Berg, and Ray.)

1. Intervention level: Primary or universal; measured effect of advisory period and computer labs.

   Design: Randomized controlled trial, randomized to individual students within each class.

Primary Intervention: Universal strength-building	Secondary Intervention: Targeted, group-level	Tertiary Intervention: Personalized counseling and other supports
Improved problem solving	Stronger attitudes against alcohol	>90% rates of voluntary use for personal guidance
Greater assertiveness	Fewer out-of-school suspensions	Reduced depression
Reduced aggressiveness	Reduced absenteeism	Fewer in-school suspensions
Greater empathy	Less tardiness	
Higher grades	Greater retention in school at 1-year follow-up (after previous failure)	

Figure 5.1. Levels of intervention.

Measurement Instrument: *California Healthy Kids* sub-scale for Resiliency Assets

- Higher scores on empathy
- Higher scores on problem solving
- High rates of voluntary use for personal guidance

2. Intervention level: Secondary or targeted; measured group-level effects in alternative and continuation schools.

   Design: Randomized controlled trials, randomized assignment to groups.

   Measurement Instruments: *Monitoring the Future* scale for alcohol and marijuana, and school administrative data for grades, attendance, behavior, and drop-out rates

   - Higher GPA
   - Greater retention in school at 1-year follow-up
   - Less tardiness (also lower absenteeism, but not significant due to non-parametric distribution)
   - Reduced aggressiveness
   - Fewer in-school suspensions
   - Fewer out-of-school suspensions
   - Stronger attitudes against alcohol
   - High rates of voluntary use for personal guidance

3. Intervention level: Tertiary or indicated; measured individual level changes for students referred for behavioral problems, in-school suspension, and detention rooms.

> Design: Quasi-experimental/comparison conditions.
> Measurement Instruments: Beck depression scale, district administrative data

- Reduced high school dropout rates
- Reduced depression scores

Implementation Structure

Ripple Effects was originally developed by Alice Ray, the originator of the *Second Step* program (see chapter 4), to address implementation fidelity challenges common to programs that depend on live teacher or consultant instruction. The Ripple Effects program is structured to make implementation easy with minimal training. Teachers are not required to become domain experts in areas they were not trained for, yet they have a clear role as facilitators. It empowers implementers to solve problems as they arise, by using staff development software that parallels the learning system in the student program, without additional training.

Because fidelity to evidence-based practices are locked in the software, the only time when instructional fidelity is compromised is if the program doesn't get used. That happens sometimes; failure to use the program is usually related to technology failure that doesn't get reported or addressed, but sometimes due to staff turnover without sufficient communication to new teachers.

Professional Development

Ripple Effects has a comprehensive suite of professional development services, which includes district level planning and consulting, live trainer training, site-specific staff training sessions, webinars, and software-based embedded coaching. Phone, web, and telecast services are included without extra fees. Implementation is supported through prebuilt tutorials and a series of manuals with background information, lesson plans, and scope and sequences for configurations linked to the tutorials. There is one manual for each level of intervention in the Ripple Effects system:

- *Universal* promotion of social-emotional competencies;
- *Targeted* prevention of substance abuse and more than a dozen common types of youth violence, including bullying, relationship abuse, and harassment;

- *Indicated* behavioral treatment plans to address disruptive and defiant behavior, and underlying causes in trauma;
- *Offense-specific interventions* for *juvenile justice* settings, from shoplifting to domestic violence;
- *Mental health interventions*, including for depression, anxiety, substance abuse;
- *Staff training* with scopes for continuous personal improvement, cultural competence and classroom management, and to sustain implementation; and
- An illustrated, "Personal Trainer for Parents" manual are also included.

Parameters for a Successful Start Up for a Local Education Agency

Successful startup of Ripple Effects for a local education agency (LEA) usually includes participation in an informational webinar, thirty-day free preview of the program by key decision-makers (including youth), some formal adoption process, a pilot test involving a purchase of a minimum of five computer-licenses of student software and parallel staff development software per school; one, four-hour, site-based training and implementation planning session; implementation of the program in at least one setting, use of RE assessment tools for pre-to post-comparisons; use of the data manager to correlate with school outcomes.

Cost Information

A single license for utilization of the Ripple Effects program software has a useful life of four to five years (see the accompanying chart of licensing fees in table 5.1). A maintenance contract enables clients to upgrade to new systems and new platforms as long as it is up to date. Access to Ripple Effects cloud-based data management system is by annual subscription.

There is a history of community, state, and national funding supports for LEA implementation of Ripple Effects. Current LEA clients have funded purchase of Ripple Effects with Title 1 (low SES), IDEA (social-emotional disorders); juvenile justice (delinquency prevention); safe and supportive school (school climate and transformation); state and county mental health, and foundation funds. NIH/NIDA funded randomized-controlled trials to evaluate efficacy.

Table 5.1. Licensing fees.

Products and Services	1 Computer License	5 Computer License	10 Computer License	30 Computer License	School-wide License
Ripple Effects Screen for Strengths (SEL Assessment)	Preview Only	$799	$1299	$1499	$1,999
Ripple Effects for Teens v4.3 (grades 6–11)	Preview Only	$2,799	$4,499	$8,199	$11,999
Ripple Effects for Kids v4.3 (grades 3–5)	Preview Only	$2,499	$3,599	$6,599	$9,199
Ripple Effects for Staff v4.3	$499	$2,499	$3,599	$6,599	$9,199
Data Management Services (Web-based)	Subscription: 10 percent of school license cost per year, plus one time set-up fee $250/school				
Live PD, Planning, Consulting, Training	$2,500/ four-hour training; $3,000 trainer training, full-day training or consultation; Normal travel expenses				

Recognition

Ripple Effects software has received twenty-nine major awards from the education, technology, health, and communications industries, including the Surgeon General's Grand Prize Award in Technology Games for Healthy Kids 2010, and the Legacy Award (ten year) from *Technology and Learning* magazine. The Company and CEO, Alice Ray, have been recognized by Business Schools at the University of Washington and University of California, Berkeley, and The National Association of Women Business owners for leadership as a social enterprise—double bottom line business.

Cautions and Critiques

Ripple Effects is an evidence-based, widely used, personalized system of mental health and social emotional supports to address both presenting behavior problems and the risk factors behind them. However, it cannot make up for an unsafe or chaotic school environment, and is not intended to replace the nuanced judgment of mental health professionals. Every topic that involves personal safety for oneself or others includes specific direction to talk to a trusted adult about the challenge being faced. A tutorial on how to access community resources, and how to talk to a counselor once you find one, is included in the program.

SUMMING UP

Initiating new programs is the approach most often chosen when educators face specific challenges or issues that they want to address. Research to prove the effectiveness of programs is also easier to do than attempting to draw conclusions about the benefit of more global or systemic efforts at school improvement because the targeted outcomes are more defined. The programs represented in this chapter all have strong evidence supporting their effectiveness, but each has a different set of objectives and each takes a different tack in how to achieve them.

The Caring School Community Program is one of the most refined, comprehensive and evidence-based programs in the SEL and prevention fields. It requires strong commitment and substantial staff training to get the promised results, including improved student discipline and increased social skills. The Playworks Program is unique in its stress on meeting children's need for safe, fun, physical activity. The wonderful surprise about the program's research results is its impact on reducing bullying and increased feelings of safety.

The Responsive Classroom Program is one of the most used and effective social skill and classroom management approaches for the elementary grades. Its adherence to rigorous teacher training standards and supports and consistently positive results has marked it as a leader in the field for more than thirty years. The Ripple Effects Program is the national leader in using technology and digital platforms to support both universal prevention and risk reduction as well as targeted assistance for students with specific behavioral or mental health related issues.

Finally, it should be said programs like the ones described here are a necessary component of a school's serious efforts to build social skills and prevent misbehavior, but are not by themselves sufficient for changing school culture and climate. Developing a prosocial school climate requires that educators carefully consider and implement a range of policy and program efforts created for the unique circumstances of their school.

Chapter Six

Targeted Approaches

THE PEER GROUP CONNECTION PROGRAM

Sherry Barr

Over the months, I've begun to notice how our actions help make an impact on the lives of the freshmen. Not only is it a pleasure to help out the freshmen with their everyday lives but it's also a way for us to learn life lessons that aren't taught in school.

—Peer leader

Program Description

Peer Group Connection (PGC) is an evidence-based, cross-age peer mentoring program that supports and eases the critical period of students' transition from middle to high school. PGC was developed by the Center for Supportive Schools (CSS) (http://www.supportiveschools.org), a nonprofit organization that works in partnership with schools. Since 1979, PGC has been implemented in more than two hundred high schools across thirteen states as well as in Asia and South America.

Purpose and Scope

There is a profound weakness in the support provided to students during the transition into high school. By the time they reach high school, as many as 40 to 60 percent of all students—urban, suburban, and rural—are "chronically disengaged" from school (Blum, 2005). Disengagement is often associated with behavior and discipline problems and may eventually lead to dropout (Fredricks, Blumenfeld, and Paris, 2004). Nearly 70 percent of the high school dropouts interviewed in the landmark 2006 study *The Silent Epidem-*

ic: Perspectives of High School Dropouts said that not feeling motivated or inspired to work hard was a major factor in their decision to drop out (Bridgeland, DiIulio, and Morison, 2006).

Research also consistently demonstrates that students are most vulnerable for dropping out of school during and immediately following their first year of high school (Cohen and Smerdon, 2009). More students fail ninth grade than any other grade and promotion rates between ninth and tenth grades are much lower than rates between other grades (Kennelly and Monrad, 2007; Wheelock and Miao, 2005). By focusing on the transition from middle to high school, this period of heightened vulnerability has the potential for being transformed into a window of opportunity for preventing the consequences of disengagement and poor decisions.

PGC taps into the power of older students to create a nurturing environment for incoming freshmen. PGC's mechanism for change is to train select school faculty to prepare older students, specifically high school juniors and seniors, to become peer leaders and mentor and educate younger students, specifically freshmen. PGC is a prosocial intervention that utilizes peer leaders to increase school engagement and reinforce desirable behaviors resulting in fewer behavior and discipline problems and improved graduation rates.

> *What has impressed me the most as I watched our peer leaders lead outreaches is how much they have grown since the start of the program. They are serious about their responsibilities and show they are genuinely committed to the academic and social success of their freshmen. They have gone the extra mile by implementing personal incentives for the freshmen to keep them motivated and engaged.*
>
> —PGC coordinator

Evidence of Effectiveness

Research History and Anticipated Outcomes

Results of a four-year, randomized control trial, conducted by researchers at Rutgers, the State University of New Jersey, with a predominantly Latino population, show that PGC participants graduated at a rate that was nine percentage points higher (77 percent versus 68 percent) than that of the control group (Johnson, Simon, and Mun, 2014). Male PGC program participants graduated at a rate of eighteen percentage points higher than males in the control group (81 percent versus 63 percent). In addition, the study found that males who exhibited a low probability for graduating at the outset of the study, but participated in PGC, had double the chance of graduating (60 percent) compared to their control group counterparts (30 percent). Consistent with this finding, males who exhibited a high probability for graduating at baseline, but did not receive PGC, graduated at a lower rate (78 percent) than males in the PGC group (91 percent).

Other research results show that as compared to students in a control or comparison group, PGC participants *outperformed their peers in four academic subjects*—English, social studies, math, and science (School District of Philadelphia, 1995); demonstrated *higher overall grades* (Hannaway and Senior, 1989); had *fewer instances of fighting* (Johnson, Pandina, and Bry, 2008); had better *school attendance* (Hannaway and Senior, 1989; Johnson, Mun, and Pandina, 2008); and *fewer discipline referrals* (Bry, Johnson, Chiong, and Urga, 2005; Hannaway and Senior, 1989).

As compared to a control or comparison group, PGC participants also score significantly higher on measures of *academic self-efficacy* (Johnson, Pandina, Bry, Powell, and Barr, 2005) and on measures that assess students' ability to *set goals* (Johnson, Mun, and Pandina, 2008); *make responsible decisions* (Johnson, Mun, and Pandina, 2008); *assert themselves* (Bry et al., 2005); *seek help* (Johnson, Mun, and Pandina, 2008; Johnson, Pandina, and Bry, 2008); *cope with problems* (Bry et al., 2005; Johnson, Pandina, and Bry, 2008); *resist peer pressure* (Johnson, Mun, and Pandina, 2008; Johnson et al., 2005); and *make friends* (Johnson, Holt, Bry, and Powell, 2008).

PGC is recognized by the National Dropout Prevention Center as a Model Program demonstrating *strong evidence of effectiveness*, its highest effectiveness rating.

Program Implementation Structure

As a school that understands the importance of promoting a positive and productive school climate, PGC has provided us with everything we were looking for: a program modeled on the idea that well-trained peer leaders are the most influential school stakeholders, high quality professional development for students and staff engaged in the program, and a high quality curriculum that leverages student-on-student interactions through weekly outreach sessions and special events with one purpose in mind—to make kids feel better about school and be more productive in school.

—High school principal

Training and Technical Assistance Model

PGC's launch in a school begins with the assembly of a *stakeholder team* of administrators, faculty, counselors, other school staff (including the school scheduler), and community members. The team is led by a coordinator, who receives the training, tools, and resources necessary to meet regularly to plan for implementation of PGC, troubleshoot obstacles, and ensure PGC's long-term sustainability.

Faculty members are carefully selected by the stakeholder team to serve as *faculty advisors*. CSS provides the stakeholder team with guidance to select faculty advisors, including criteria such as: enthusiasm for PGC and a peer leadership approach to high school transition support; commitment to positive youth development; ability to work collaboratively with others; willingness to implement PGC model with fidelity; and willingness to team-teach the PGC course with a colleague and to utilize a facilitation model. Faculty advisors participate in an eleven-day intensive train-the-trainer course over a one-and-a-half-year period to learn how to run the program and teach junior and senior peer leaders in the daily leadership course. Faculty advisors also participate in on-site coaching sessions provided by CSS staff.

Juniors and seniors are carefully selected by faculty advisors to become *peer leaders* and serve as mentors for ninth graders. Criteria for selection includes a clear commitment to the role of mentor; ability to work collaboratively with others; friendliness; appeal to younger students as a role-model; and self-confidence. Students must also demonstrate adequate academic performance, strong attendance at school, and no serious discipline infractions. CSS supports faculty advisors to select a diverse group of peer leaders that accurately reflects the racial/ethnic composition of the school community, neighborhood affiliation, socioeconomic status, affiliation with known cliques, and an equal number of girls and boys.

> *What impresses me is the connection that is made among the peer leaders. These students see themselves as critical partners in their own success as well as the success of others and ultimately the school. Student leaders who are empowered to become leaders within their school develop skills that better prepare them for college and the world of work. Student mentees experience a caring and student-focused school that provides support necessary for them to discuss difficulties in both society as well as within their personal lives . . . these elements are necessary components within a caring community. They set a tone and provide a purpose to our community of learners.*
>
> *—Principal*

Peer leaders are trained and conduct weekly outreach sessions as part of their regular school schedule in a *daily, forty-five-minute leadership development class* typically offered as an elective course for credit. Within the daily class, peer leaders receive four days of training for every one day of mentoring they provide to freshmen. This helps peer leaders prepare to lead their groups each week and debrief following each session, sharing successes, challenges, and suggestions for handling issues. As a school-based program that is integrated into the school day, PGC provides a built-in mechanism for retaining participants in contrast to extracurricular models that are vulnerable to a variety of scheduling, transportation, and commitment challenges.

CSS works closely with faculty advisors to assign students to *peer groups*. PGC is designed to reach all freshmen in a school. PGC typically replaces one day per week of physical education (PE) for freshmen in participating high schools. CSS also provides a structured, two-hour protocol for co-leader selection and assignment to lead peer groups (i.e., co-leader teams should be male/female and complement one another's skills and interests). CSS works closely with administrators and staff beginning prior to program implementation to coordinate scheduling.

Peer leaders work in pairs to co-lead groups of ten to fourteen freshmen in *outreach sessions* once each week during the school day in which the freshmen participate in engaging, hands-on activities and simulations. In peer groups, freshmen spend approximately six weeks engaged in activities designed to help students get to know one another, build a cohesive group, and set ground rules for working together. Following this, sessions focus on skill development through *experiential learning* activities.

Skills addressed throughout the PGC curriculum include goal setting, decision making, and help seeking skills. During the second half of the year, peer leaders and their freshman peer groups research, plan, and execute a *service learning* project which reinforces the skills learned during the first half of the year and promotes a sense of connectedness to the school and community

LEA Requirements for Successful Start-Up

There are several pre-implementation tasks that must be completed to ensure successful program implementation, including: selecting appropriate faculty advisors; scheduling the weekly freshman outreach sessions; recruiting, selecting and scheduling peer leaders for the daily leadership course; identifying appropriate physical space in the building for the multiple peer groups to meet; and obtaining school-wide faculty buy-in for the program. Convening a committed team of stakeholders to focus on the successful execution of these tasks is essential.

Sustaining the Program over Time

PGC is designed to be integrated into the school day and sustained in perpetuity. PGC taps into existing school resources such as staff, students, and time in the school day: (1) PGC *trains existing school faculty members* rather than requiring nonschool or additional school staff; (2) PGC *taps into older students*, an underutilized resource in school improvement efforts, to train and support younger students; (3) PGC *ensures peer leaders receive rigorous training* through a credit-bearing leadership course to prepare them to be mentors; and (4) PGC is *integrated into the school day* increasing the likelihood that it becomes institutionalized and sustained over time.

One of the greatest threats to the sustainability of PGC is administrative and staff turnover, especially principal turnover. To mitigate this risk, sufficient time must be invested up front to establish and train the stakeholder team of administrators, faculty, counselors, other school staff, and community members who provide a broad base of support for the program and mitigate potential risks due to turnover of one or more key individuals.

Availability and Cost

PGC requires a one-time initial investment and a recurring cost of only a few dollars per student per year, yet has the potential to leverage significant impact for decades to come by providing each new cohort of incoming ninth-grade students with the evidenced-based support they need to transition successfully into high school, excel in school, and graduate on time.

Schools pay a one-time fee to CSS to provide all training and technical assistance necessary for stakeholders and faculty advisors to effectively launch PGC. Training and technical assistance addresses key programmatic issues such as scheduling and other logistics; selecting faculty advisors and peer leaders; teaching the peer leadership class; and experiencing, firsthand, the freshman outreach activities. The cost for the start-up support is influenced by the number of freshman participants.

Ongoing costs that a school incurs to implement PGC include an annual overnight three-day, two-night leadership development retreat for peer leaders, classroom materials, food for special events, including family nights, and materials for service learning projects. These costs typically range per year from $3,000 to $7,000 and are often covered through in-kind contributions.

Schools and local education agencies (LEAs) often cover the costs associated with launching and sustaining PGC from their school budgets. Funding support for PGC is also sought through federal and state government, foundation, and corporate grants.

Cautions and Critiques

Introducing PGC into a new high school requires upfront collaboration among school stakeholders and CSS staff to ensure program sustainability and, in turn, cost effectiveness. Time must be invested to establish and train the stakeholder team who provides a broad base of support for the program and mitigates potential risks due to turnover of one or more key individuals.

Time is also required to effectively integrate PGC into the school day and address scheduling challenges that could impact proper implementation.

It is also critical for schools to select faculty advisors who are enthusiastic and committed to the program's goals, are able to attend all program training, and are committed to implementing the program with fidelity to the model. In addition, peer leaders need to be enthusiastic and credible ambassadors for the program and exhibit positive role modeling characteristics. Careful attention to widely publicizing the opportunity to become a peer leader to the pool of eligible students is likely to lead to a group of peer leaders who are representative of the larger student body.

ALTERNATIVE EDUCATION PROGRAMS

Robert Eichorn

Throughout the world, nontraditional and alternative schools serve students who require or thrive in an environment other than a traditional educational setting. This population of learners may face challenges in school, home, and community. As a result, their ability to access services in the traditional setting may be at-risk. Nontraditional and alternative education delivers innovative twenty-first-century approaches to teaching and learning which provides students with the opportunity to meet graduation requirements, engage in college and career readiness, and participate as productive members of their communities.

For decades, nontraditional and alternative schools have increased student achievement, changed the lives of at-risk students, and fostered an increased sense of community for all stakeholders. When adopted and implemented with fidelity, alternative schools can transform school districts (Raywid, 1994). While local education agencies have been at the forefront of alternative school creation and program improvement, individual states have developed an increased role with oversight and program support. The Wisconsin Department of Education (n.d.) notes that alternatives must be developed due to the fact that large or traditional school environments do not meet the needs of all students, particularly those who are at at-risk, vulnerable, or disengaged from the instructional process.

Evidence-Based Practice Standards

Research conducted by the National Alternative Education Association (NAEA) has identified fifteen exemplary practices for creating, implementing, and sustaining high quality nontraditional and alternative schools. *Exemplary Practices 2.0: Standards of Quality and Program Evaluation 2014* (NAEA, n.d.) provides educational leaders and practitioners with a standards-based approach to program evaluation, identifies essential characteristics, and notes the importance of wrap-around services that include school counseling, social work, and technology. All of these services play a role in developing and implementing successful alternative schools and programs.

According to the NAEA, when incorporated into alternative school design the fifteen exemplary practices assure high quality educational services are delivered with fidelity, academic standards, and benchmarks are adhered to consistently, and student achievement is the foundation for program evaluation. These include, a school formulated vision and mission, experienced leadership, stakeholder ownership of climate and school culture, ongoing professional development, and rigorous and relevant traditional, digital, and blended curriculum. In addition, consistent and authentic student assessment, followed by multiyear transition planning which includes parents and community stakeholders are essential components for effective alternative schools. Moreover, strategic collaboration with community agencies led by professional school counselors and social workers is essential in developing a nontraditional education plan for each student. Each of these components should contain specific benchmarks and indicators schools can use to plan, reflect, and evaluate program performance.

Examples of the Standard's Utilization and Efficacy

LEAs as well as state departments of education have been adopting the exemplary practices outlined above as part of their rubric for existing program monitoring and evaluation. In Virginia, Prince William County Public Schools alternative high school, New Directions, embraced the fifteen standards and indicators, increased enrollment by 300 percent, and raised graduation rates by 19 percent with the last four consecutive years of 90 percent or better graduation rates. As a result, the district's on-time graduation rate increased to 90 percent in 2014.

The Tennessee Department of Education has adopted the *NAEA Exemplary Practices* and created a Governor's Advisory Council for Alternative Education. The council, which includes members of the NAEA, is charged with reviewing issues, appraising plans, assessing curricula, and evaluating rules of governance as each relates to nontraditional and alternative schools. This systemic approach at the local and state level serves to provide a common structure to ensure students and those that serve them are provided with the human, capital, and technical resources to create and maintain exemplary schools. In addition, *Exemplary Practices 2.0* informs school districts, divisions, communities, and their stakeholders on the critical "look fors" that should be evident in nontraditional or alternative schools and found in the school community that supports each program.

Colleges and universities offering alternative education degree and certificate programs that emphasize NAEA Exemplary Practices include Lock Haven University, University of Wisconsin, and University of West Florida. LEAs should check to see what standards for alternative programs exist in their states, benchmarking them against the Exemplary Practice standards, and utilize the aforementioned resources to develop their programs.

Support and Technical Assistance

Support and technical assistance is offered through a variety of mechanisms for alternative and nontraditional educators. The NAEA holds annual multi-day professional development conferences, which provide continuing education units to attendees and helps create and support state alternative education associations. Organization leaders visit and provide programmatic feedback to existing and developing schools throughout the United States. The Oklahoma Technical Assistance Center is an example of state-level technical assistance. Since 1978, it has served school districts in the state with an emphasis on closing the achievement gap and reducing the dropout rate. State and local education agencies have engaged in partnerships with organizations of different types from both the public and private sectors to provide professional development opportunities that target program development, student achievement, and educator support through the review of student performance data.

Effective benchmarking of state and local alternative education standards against the NAEA standards will lead to the creation of model programs that increase student achievement, are cost effective, and regionally aligned. While per pupil costs vary by jurisdiction, effective schools and programs can be created using the standard allocation model utilized for traditional schools. In order to maintain at least a recommended twelve-to-one student ratio using this allocation model, flexible schedules can be implemented along with blended instruction to maximize enrollment while maintaining small class size.

In addition, operating multiple academic shifts on abbreviated schedules takes full advantage of the per pupil allocation and enrollment opportunities, particularly at the high school level. For example, utilizing two three-hour academic shift sessions with digital learning as a complement affords a student the opportunity to earn eight academic credits in a year on a half-day schedule. As a result, students can then engage in employment, internship, or other off-campus activities.

Funding Alternative Education Programs and Schools

Historically, funding streams for alternative programs come in the form of grant opportunities from the state or federal level. For example, the Commonwealth of Virginia provides grants to regional alternative programs for staffing purposes. This affords multiple districts to subsequently refer students for educational services. In addition, federal grants such the 21st Century Community Learning Centers provide traditional schools the opportunity to staff after school tutorial and as well as "school-within-a-school" programs to support the needs of disenfranchised and at-risk youth. This opportunity, funded through the Elementary and Secondary Education of 1965 (ESEA) and as amended by the No Child Left Behind Act of 2001 (NCLB) is designed to assist students in meeting or exceeding the local or state standards in core content subject areas. While accessing a range of state and national grant opportunities can provide added value and resources to any traditional or alternative school, it should be noted a consistent local funding stream is critical to the success and long term viability of any alternative school or program.

Creating and sustaining high performing alternative schools can be accomplished when LEA leadership focus on an outcomes-based approach throughout the developmental process. Emphasis should be front-end planning with a shared vision supported by the superintendent and school board. In particular, human, capital, and technical resources should be aligned based on the performance data of the target student population.

In addition to achievement data, program surveys should be distributed to stakeholders with an emphasis on community, economic, and logistical needs of the families and students served by the alternative school. The most economically needy, emotionally starved, and academically challenged students deserve the best teachers and resources.

A Cautionary Tale

When adequate planning and support is absent, which is not uncommon, historically, in the United States, the positive results referenced earlier do not accrue, placing the programs in jeopardy. The following scenario is typical of this pattern: An alternative program is created for the most at-risk students in a school district in a less than adequate facility. Staffing is minimal and the educators and other staff hired are not adequately trained or skilled in working with the challenges associated with alternative students. The program is underfunded and not provided with equitable resources found in traditional schools. The result: the school typically exists two to three years, has poor academic achievement results, a high turnover rate for staff, and subsequently closes due to performance and funding challenges.

Because of the need for alternative education placements for students who are not succeeding in more traditional schools, it is not atypical that, after an alternative school fails, because of the kind of factors described above, a year later, a new school or program is opened in the same LEA. However, if the same process is followed the same result will occur. Engaging stakeholders and providing equitable resources at the onset of a new alternative school or a school in crisis that is in transformation will eliminate the cautionary tale. It will create opportunities for students and change the landscape for the entire school district.

Resources

Contact the National Alternative Education Association through their Web site at http://the-naea.org/NAEA/.

SUMMING UP

Targeted approaches to building a prosocial school climate take many forms. Some programs highlighted in earlier chapters, such as Restorative Practices, PBIS, and Ripple Effects, for example, address students who exhibit the most severe behavior problems in the school context. This chapter uses the term to highlight two very different kinds of approaches, one a preventive program, and the other a whole-school setting model dedicated to addressing the needs of these students.

The Peer Group Connections Program is the premier evidence-based program that empowers positive peer group learning and social skill development in early adolescents. It focuses on times of transition and the developmental period when peer groups are the most powerful. Alternative education programs are common in most large school districts as the way to create a learning environment that responds to the special needs of students whose family and personal histories have resulted in problems in adjusting to traditional school environments that typically result in disciplinary issues.

Chapter Seven

School Profiles

Different Approaches to Establishing Prosocial Discipline

Philip M. Brown with Eight School Leaders

The eight schools profiled below each have a unique history regarding how they manage their student behavior and discipline issues. They have been chosen as examples to learn from through recommendations from colleagues and the national recognition they have received from a number of different sources, including Character.org, the Collaborative for Academic, Social, and Emotional Learning, and the Graduate School of Education at the University of Virginia. They all have seen positive behavioral changes in their students as a result of their efforts as well as reduction in discipline problems.

What follows is basic information about the schools and a brief highlight describing one or more aspects of their approaches and programs that have proven successful. Fuller descriptions of their process and programs can be found on the Web site of the National School Climate Center, which has generously agreed to host this portion of the book on their Web site. Go to www.schoolclimate.org and look for "School Discipline Profiles."

LEATAATA FLOYD ELEMENTARY SCHOOL (LFE)

Basic Description

LFE is a neighborhood elementary school with 350 students serving the Seavey Circle and New Helvetia neighborhoods in the Sacramento City, California's Unified School District. For many years LFE has had the highest referral/suspension/expulsion rate in the district while having the lowest daily attendance percentage. It is currently in year four of "priority" status under the U.S. Department of Education's "turnaround school" designation system for low-performing schools.

Highlight

Historically, this school was created as a segregated school that targeted specific subgroups of students within the district. After having been designated a failing "turn around school" under the NCLB guidelines, the staff of Leataata Floyd decided to focus on three prosocial practices of inclusive pedagogy to address the most significant needs of the students and families: Social-Emotional Learning (SEL), Positive Behavioral and Intervention and Support (PBIS), and Restorative Justice (RJ). Their simple starting point included three principles around which they oriented their work:

1. Kids have to like school;
2. Students and parents/guardians must develop trust and confidence in the school; and
3. These two needs must be directly addressed while academic needs are attended to.

MARCUS GARVEY ELEMENTARY SCHOOL

Basic Description

Marcus Garvey School is a pre-K through eighth grade elementary school with approximately three hundred students located in the Washington Heights Neighborhood on the South Side of Chicago, Illinois. It serves children who live in the immediate neighborhood. Ninety-four percent of the students qualify for free or reduced price lunches, and all are African American.

Highlight

Marcus Garvey has partnered with the Collaborative for Academic, Social and Emotional Learning and adopted an evidence-based SEL program, *Second Step*, to teach behavior and social skills. In addition to classroom instruction, every staff member (including the administrators) is assigned a group of eight to twelve students from different grade levels, and each week begins with a twenty-minute period of reflection and skill building on topics that are organized monthly by the key SEL objectives. Through the use of these strategies, the school has been successful in assisting students to take greater responsibility for managing and controlling their own behavior.

STEWARTSVILLE ELEMENTARY SCHOOL

Basic Description

Stewartsville Elementary School is a pre-K to fifth grade school with 430 students in rural Goodview, Virginia, nestled in the foothills of the Blue Ridge Mountains. Sixty-eight percent of its largely white student body qualify for free or reduced lunch.

Highlight

When Principal Susan Mele arrived in 2010 student behavior was completely out of control and discipline was in chaos. She chose to implement an evidence-based program, the *Responsive Classroom*. Within a year of implementation and staff buy-in, teachers began to change their attitudes about how they looked at the children they taught, and this had profound effects on their behavior. Where teachers previously felt helpless and frustrated and felt that nothing would work, they now enjoy their jobs more, which is evident through the supportive language they used with the children. Discipline referrals dropped by 75 percent and academic test scores began increasing.

CHARLES BOEHM MIDDLE SCHOOL

Basic Description

Charles Boehm Middle School serves 730 students in grades six through eight and is located in Yardley, Pennsylvania. It is one of three middle schools in the Pennsbury School District serving two boroughs and two townships in the suburbs of Philadelphia, Pennsylvania. The majority of students (82 percent) report that they are Caucasian, 0.2 percent English language learners (ELL), 22 percent socioeconomically disadvantaged, and 20 percent receiving special education services.

Highlight

Following teacher surveys of discipline issues, Charles Boehm introduced a combination of positive behavioral support and character education programs that are designed as a system to increase intrinsic motivation in students throughout middle school. School discipline referrals and suspension are down and the school has been recognized as a National School of Character.

CHERRY HILL ALTERNATIVE HIGH SCHOOL

Basic Description

The Cherry Hill, New Jersey, School District's Alternative High School is a replacement program for at-promise students in grades nine to twelve. Approximately 65 percent of its forty-four special education–classified students are Caucasian, 20 percent black/African American, and 15 percent Hispanic/Latino. Forty-one percent of the school's students are eligible for free or reduced lunch.

Highlight

While on the surface this school might appear similar to many alternative education settings, the principal and staff tell a powerful story of their journey in changing the culture of the building over the past six years. The school adopted the *Nurtured Heart Approach Model for Educators*, as a common lens and language in furthering their commitment to build the character of each student in a personal and individualized way, and uses a professional learning communities model for continued staff development and school improvement. The path taken by two different principals and the staff resulted in better attendance, discipline, academic improvement, and the school being recognized as a National School of Character.

LAKE BRADDOCK SECONDARY SCHOOL

Basic Description

Lake Braddock Secondary School (LBSS), located in Burke, Virginia, is part of the Washington, DC, suburban sprawl, and one of three secondary schools (combined middle and high school) in the Fairfax County Public Schools—the twelfth largest school system in the country. The school is the largest in Virginia, currently enrolling over four thousand students in grades seven through twelve. The school has 12.8 percent of its students receiving special education services, and 16.2 percent of students receive free or reduced priced meals. Additionally, 7.2 percent of students are identified as limited English proficient. The school's white (non-Hispanic) population is the largest student group at 52.7 percent.

Highlight

Starting in the 2014–2015 school year Fairfax County Public Schools created a new position in all twenty-five high schools called "System of Support

Advisor" (SOSA). The position coordinates continuing professional development, and prevention programs and in-school intervention opportunities for students in the discipline process. The intention is to provide strategies, language, and behavioral options to help students effectively manage challenges and frustrations.

The SOSA uses PBIS and Response to Intervention models to reduce behavior incidents, reduce recidivism rates, and respond to student behavior issues, as well as to build whole-school teacher capacity to respond to behavioral issues. In order to promote positive approaches to discipline Lake Bradock's SOSA has also received additional training in conflict resolution, peer mediation, and restorative justice practices.

SCARSDALE ALTERNATIVE SCHOOL

Basic Description

The Scarsdale Alternative School, known as the A School, is a satellite of the larger public suburban school, Scarsdale High School in New York, and enrolls eighty-two students in the tenth through twelfth grades. Students of this National School of Character apply to be part of a program that includes disaffected, gifted, average, and learning disabled students with a balance of boys and girls.

Highlight

The A School was founded as a Just Community School in 1972 and dedicated itself to promoting moral growth. A host of democratically informed processes such as Agenda, Core Group, Internship, and Community Meeting are closely linked structures designed to push students to enhance their perspective taking and other prosocial skills.

The Fairness Committee determines consequences for those who do not abide by the school's rules and norms. It consists of a representative group of students including one trained student facilitator who leads the case. A teacher also sits on the case as a voting member of the committee. The task of the Fairness Committee is to hear and decide cases of alleged rule violations such as cheating, bullying, use of drugs, and disrespect of fellow community members.

JEROME HARRISON ELEMENTARY SCHOOL

Basic Description

Jerome Harrison Elementary School is a suburban pre-K–2 school located in a predominately middle-class community in North Branford, Connecticut. The student population of 412 is represented by 94 percent white/Caucasian and the remaining 6 percent includes Asian, Black, Hispanic, and Indian. The special education population is roughly 10 percent, an ELL population of 2 percent, and free and reduced lunch socioeconomic status classification of 18 percent and rising.

Highlight

This elementary school principal led the North Branford School District in establishing a Threat Assessment Program as part of a broader approach to school climate improvement and prosocial disciplinary practices. The profile provides a practical example of how one local district and school came to realize what they needed to change and how they made progress over the course of a year in a way that was proactive and supportive of existing positive school climate measures.

Chapter Eight

The U.S. Department of Education's Guiding Principles on School Discipline

SUMMARY

Jessica Savage

In an effort to create the safe, supportive, and positive environments that students need in order to learn and thrive, schools frequently rely on the use of exclusionary discipline practices, notably suspensions and expulsions. However, according to data from the U.S. Department of Education's Office for Civil Rights (OCR), instead of making schools safer and more engaging environments, the prevalent use of exclusionary discipline practices, which disproportionately affects students of color and students with disabilities, actually detracts from school environments and negatively impacts students (U.S. Department of Education, 2014).

According to OCR, the "widespread overuse" of exclusionary discipline practices directly undermines efforts to create the positive school climate required for students to feel engaged in school and comes at a tremendous cost. In particular, when students are removed from the classroom it typically means they have numerous unsupervised daytime hours and they fail to receive both the academic benefit of an education as well as the social benefits of peer interactions and adult mentorship.

Moreover, removing students from school does not offer them the skills and techniques required to improve their misbehavior and avoid repeating it, so it is a limited strategy that may benefit the school, but harms the student. Increased suspension rates are associated with an increased likelihood of repeating a grade, dropping out of school and involvement in the juvenile justice system, and decreased standardized test scores and school wide academic achievement (U.S. Department of Education, 2014).

The Guiding Principles

In light of this data, and based on the belief that in order for there to be effective teaching and learning schools must have both safe and supportive environments, the U.S. Department of Education (DOE) called on state, district, and school leaders "to proactively redesign discipline policies and practices to more effectively foster supportive and safe school climates" (U.S. Department of Education, 2014, ii). The DOE determined that schools that are safe and successful typically achieve this condition through utilizing a number of common approaches. Synthesizing these approaches, the DOE identified three Guiding Principles that policymakers, district officials, school leaders, and key stakeholders should consider when working to improve the climate and discipline policies and practices in schools.

In the "Guiding Principles" document the DOE provides a resource guide for improving school climate and discipline presented through three Guiding Principles, along with Action Steps, relevant research, and resources that can be used to achieve them.[1] Below is a summary of the three Guiding Principles and the Action Steps that accompany them.

Guiding Principle 1: Create a Positive Climate and Focus on Prevention

Guiding Principle 1 calls on schools to create positive school climates and focus on preventing problem behaviors before they occur so that all students—in particular those who are struggling and at risk—can be engaged and learn. It suggests six Action Steps that schools can take in order to improve the climate of a school.

Action Step 1 instructs schools to make an intentional effort to create a more positive school climate through garnering input from the entire school community to develop "climate goals" that align with the school's academic goals. It suggests that schools consider including goals that are targeted toward providing support for students who may be at risk for dropping out of school or other behavioral problems. In addition, it suggests that schools utilize comprehensive needs assessments to identify areas that need improvement and that schools establish formal structures and procedures that support the collection and monitoring of school climate data. Some examples of such supports include developing "school-based climate teams" that involve all members of the school community, and assigning personnel to be in charge of dealing with complaints and students' concerns.

Action Step 2 involves promoting positive student behavior through prioritizing the use of evidence-based prevention strategies, such as tiered supports,[2] and providing developmentally and behaviorally appropriate interventions to students identified as at-risk. Integral to this Action Step is having trained school-based support personnel who can partner with teachers to help them recognize student needs and provide support to struggling and at-risk students.

Action Step 3 discusses promoting students' social and emotional skills to support academic achievement, positive behavior, and a positive school climate. The DOE based this Action Step on the wealth of research showing that building noncognitive competencies, such as self-awareness, self-management, and resilience, can help students in a host of ways, including supporting healthy interpersonal relationships, pursuing goals, and academic success and social development.

In Action Step 4, schools are directed to provide all school-based personnel with regular training and support concerning how to engage students and support positive behavior. This Action Step sets forth that professional development should include coaching on how to maintain a positive school climate and should emphasize strategies and concepts for ensuring that all students are treated fairly, such as conflict resolution strategies, cultural responsiveness, and civil rights laws. In addition, schools are instructed to utilize assessments to measure the staff's growth and to ensure that the professional development is in fact achieving its goal of improving school climate.

Action Step 5 involves forming collaborations and partnerships between all stakeholders, including local mental health agencies, law enforcement, juvenile justice agencies, and child welfare, in order to ensure that all resources, prevention efforts, and intervention programs complement each other and thus more effectively and appropriately support students.

Action Step 6 outlines the roles, expectations, and appropriate use of school-based law enforcement officers. Noting that arrests and referrals to law enforcement negatively impact students and that students of color and those with disabilities have disproportionately more contact with the justice system, Action Step 6 sets forth that the role of school-based law enforcement officers should be focused on improving safety and decreasing inappropriate referrals to law enforcement; they should not become involved in routine school disciplinary matters.

These expectations should be clearly documented in written policies or memoranda of understanding (MOUs) and schools should provide officers with rigorous training so they understand these expectations and are capable of carrying them out. Action Step 6 also provides specific instructions regarding the use of law enforcement as a response to school discipline problems and instructs schools to provide training to their staff so that everyone understands when and how to involve law enforcement in discipline matters. Furthermore, schools are instructed to closely monitor the use of school-based law enforcement officers and use the data as part of a continuous process of improvement.

Guiding Principle 2: Develop Clear, Appropriate, and Consistent
Expectations and Consequences to Address Disruptive Student Behaviors

Guiding Principle 2 calls on schools to provide students with discipline policies and codes of conduct that have "clear, appropriate, and consistently applied expectations" (U.S. Department of Education, 2014, 11) regarding behavior and consequences for misbehavior. Guiding Principle 2 includes five Actions Steps.

Action Step 1 specifies that school discipline policies should set high and positive expectations for behavior and that these expectations should be clearly communicated to all students. In addition, schools should utilize an instructional approach to school discipline that not only holds those who bully accountable but also teaches students to learn from their misbehavior, grow, and achieve academically.

Action Step 2 instructs schools to include multiple stakeholders within the school community, such as families, students, and school personnel, in the development and implementation of discipline policies and codes of conduct. In addition, schools should regularly and clearly share the policies with the school community and, when disciplinary incidents arise, have protocols and due process requirements in place to ensure parents and guardians are promptly notified.

Action Step 3 directs schools to have "clear, developmentally appropriate, and proportional consequences" (U.S. Department of Education, 2014, 13) for misbehavior and suggests that zero-tolerance discipline policies may prevent this from occurring. In addition, it sets forth that responses to misbehavior generally should *not* include involving law enforcement.

Action Step 4 instructs schools to comply with their federal and state laws and ensure that, in both policy and practice, they include appropriate discipline procedures for students with disabilities. In addition, schools are told to ensure that their discipline policies provide due process protections for all students.

Action Step 5 discusses the negative consequences of suspending and excluding students for misbehavior and instructs schools to remove students from the classroom only as a last resort. In addition, it sets forth that, in the event that a student does need to be removed, schools should provide that student with an alternative setting in which to receive academic instruction, and students should return to their regular class room as soon as possible.

Guiding Principle 3: Ensure Fairness, Equity, and Continuous Improvement

Guiding Principle 3 calls on schools to "ensure fairness, equity, and continuous improvement" in the implementation and use of school discipline policies and practices (U.S. Department of Education, 2014, 16). Guiding Principle 3 states that this can best be accomplished through building staff capacity and continuously evaluating the school's discipline policies and practices. It suggests two Action Steps for schools to follow.

Action Step 1 instructs schools to equip all school staff with the training and skills that will allow them to be able to utilize school discipline policies to respond to misconduct in a fair, equitable, and nondiscriminatory manner that does not disproportionately target students of color, students with disabilities, or at-risk students. Similarly, it sets forth that schools need to understand their legal obligations under the federal civil rights laws.

Action Step 2 directs schools to proactively work to prevent, recognize, and eliminate discriminatory discipline and its unintended consequences through regularly collecting and analyzing data, including feedback from the entire school community, and evaluating their discipline policies and practices. Schools are instructed to use data, analysis, and community feedback in order to develop action plans and continuously modify policies and practices and provide support as needed.

Conclusion

Working to create positive school climates as well as fair and equitable discipline policies and practices are efforts that go hand-in-hand. Both are critical steps for increasing academic achievement and having a student body that feels safe, engaged, and ready to succeed. In the document discussed above, the DOE identified three guiding principles that educational leaders should consider when striving to improve school climate and discipline policies and practices: "(1) Create positive climates and focus on prevention; (2) Develop clear, appropriate, and consistent expectations and consequences to address disruptive student behaviors; and (3) Ensure fairness, equity and continuous improvement" (U.S. Department of Education, 2014, 1).

Following these principles is an important first step toward improving discipline policies and practices in states and districts. Only through doing so will educational leaders be able to provide *all* students with safe and productive learning environments and achieve their goal of improving the school climate and promoting academic excellence in their schools.

THE IMPACT OF THE U.S. DEPARTMENT OF EDUCATION DISCIPLINE GUIDELINES: UNDERSTANDING, LIABILITY, AND RESPONSIBLE ACTION

David Nash

On October 11, 2011, the U.S. Departments of Education and Justice jointly announced "the successful resolution of the first proactive civil rights enforcement action taken by the Department of Education under the Obama Administration." The settlement required the district to "eliminate inequitable and disproportionate discipline practices" regarding African American students and to increase access to high-level educational opportunities for both African American and Latino students.[3]

On December 18, 2012, the U.S. Department of Education (USDOE) and U.S. Department of Justice (DOJ) announced the settlement of a "significant, proactive civil rights enforcement action" involving the Christina School District, the largest school district in the state of Delaware, which required the district to "implement disciplinary practices that will effectively promote equity in discipline."[4]

Then on January 8, 2014, the USDOE and DOJ announced the release of a comprehensive guidance package to assist school districts in meeting their legal obligations to administer student discipline without discriminating on the basis of race, color, or national origin. The package includes a *Dear Colleague Letter* that provides districts with a legal framework and examples of scenarios to assist educators in applying the law.[5]

The importance of this guidance package was underscored in the remarks of the education secretary and the attorney general. Education Secretary Arne Duncan stressed that "racial discrimination in school discipline is a real problem today, and not just an issue from forty or fifty years ago."[6] Added Attorney General Eric Holder, "students of color and those with disabilities often receiv[e] different and more severe punishment than their peers," and are being victimized by the "school-to-prison pipeline."[7]

What these actions tell us is that we have entered a new age of civil rights enforcement in our schools—an age in which key federal agencies are acting proactively to investigate and address overall disparities in student discipline rates, rather than simply responding piecemeal to individual allegations of discrimination.

Whether we are ready or not, the U.S. Departments of Education and Justice have shone a spotlight—an uncomfortably bright spotlight—on an issue that has plagued our nation's schools for too long. Simply put, our collective approach to student discipline as a nation has resulted in wildly varying discipline rates for students based on factors such as race, ethnicity, and disability.[8]

As the USDOE and DOJ have pointed out in their recent *Dear Colleague Letter*, this punitive approach is not sustainable, either as educational or economic policy; not in a nation where our economic future depends on our ability to compete internationally and maximize the talents and abilities of all students, regardless of race, ethnicity, or disability.[9] The USDOE and DOJ *Dear Colleague Letter* makes clear that this is also a critical legal issue.[10] School districts that fail to muster the courage to tackle this issue according to the USDOE guidelines outlined below face the prospect of potential liability in addition to the disservice to their affected students. Without appropriate action, expenditures resulting from litigation could well begin to consume a significant portion of resources that would be better spent on improving educational opportunities for all students.

Understanding the Legal Framework

The USDOE and DOJ letter provides the legal framework for schools to use in seeking to determine whether or not a given student discipline practice is illegal, under Titles IV and VI of the Civil Rights Act of 1964. A similar analysis applies to alleged discrimination based on gender, disability, or religion.[11] The first step is determining what category an alleged discriminatory discipline practice falls into. There are two broad categories of discrimination to consider—*Differential Treatment* (intentional discrimination) and *Disparate Impact* (unintentional but having the unjustified effect of discriminating). Each has its own, slightly different legal analysis.[12]

Differential Treatment Analysis

For differential treatment cases, the essential legal questions are:

1. Was a student denied an educational benefit? (If suspended or expelled, the answer would be "Yes.")
2. Were similarly situated students not of the same race (or other protected characteristic) treated differently?
3. Can the school offer a legitimate, nondiscriminatory reason for its actions?
4. Is the reason offered a pretext for discrimination?

When it comes to differential treatment, where there is a school staff member (or even a volunteer) engaging in intentional discrimination, it is often the result of fear, unconscious biases, or lack of education. The good news is that these are all causes that can be addressed through professional development. In addition, the discriminatory intent of one or a few staff members is generally not shared by other staff members in that school community. Thus, purposeful discrimination is generally the exception, not the rule.

How do we determine if the actions of school officials are the result of discriminatory intent? It is important to note that we rarely have the "smoking gun," or outright admissions of discriminatory intent. What is more common is the discipline policy that is neutral regarding factors such as race on its face, but is administered in a discriminatory manner, or in a manner that gives wide discretion to individual staff members; discretion which may be used to promote discriminatory ends. [13]

For example, consider the scenario where a school district has a policy that allows for a one-day suspension for "acting in a threatening manner." Assume further that statistical data shows that African American students are suspended at a disproportionate rate under this district's policy. Further investigation shows that African American students are more likely than other students to be suspended under this policy for congregating in groups in hallways, a behavior that is common among all students. The result? If the district cannot offer a legitimate, nondiscriminatory reason for its differential treatment, it will be guilty of engaging in racial discrimination. [14]

This is a classic example of a case in which a well-intentioned, but overly broad, and poorly defined policy can result in discriminatory implementation, perhaps because some teaching staff members feel more threatened when African American students gather in groups. As part of the remedy in a case such as this, the district would likely be required to develop a clearly defined definition of "threatening behavior," complete with examples of what would be considered threatening actions, and would be required to provide training for staff on issues such as effective behavior interventions and cultural sensitivity. [15]

A key aspect of the legal analysis for differential treatment cases involves a review of whether *similarly situated* students were treated differently and whether there is a pattern to this differential treatment that can be linked to a protected characteristic such as race, ethnicity, or disability. In order to determine this, it is often necessary to look beyond a specific incident and examine how a school handled prior incidents involving similar behavior. Essentially, it means that one allegation of racial discrimination could result in a school having to defend its actions on a much larger scale, taking into account its handling of a large number of prior incidents. Thus, it becomes critical for school officials to proactively determine if unexplainable disciplinary patterns exist, *before* a legal dispute arises.

Disparate Impact Analysis

For disparate impact allegations, the essential legal questions are different. They are:

1. Has the discipline policy resulted in an adverse impact on students of a particular race (or other protected characteristic)?
2. If so, is the discipline policy necessary to meet an important educational goal?
3. If the policy is necessary to meet an important educational goal, are there comparable policies or practices that would meet the same goal with less of a negative impact on students of a particular race?

As with differential treatment, this is a good news / bad news analysis. The bad news is that data from the USDOE suggests that a majority of schools across the nation are engaging in disciplinary practices that have a negative, disparate impact on students based on race and other protected characteristics. The good news is that disparate impact has nothing to do with intent. In many cases, schools are unintentionally engaging in school discipline practices that result in a disparate impact, but in fact have no desire to discriminate in any way. This intention-result gap creates an opportunity that school officials should embrace—the opportunity to bring together well-intentioned, caring, intelligent stakeholders from all aspects of the school community to overcome these unintentional outcomes and expand opportunities for all students to succeed.

Moving Forward: Embracing Best Practices and Minimizing Legal Liability

For school officials—principals, superintendents, elected leaders, and educators—seeking to engage in meaningful efforts to address the issue of discipline equity, it is difficult to know where to begin. One wrong step in discussing such a hot button issue could lead to community anger and mistrust, mar the district's image, and put careers in jeopardy. But the consequences of ignoring the problem are even worse—unjust discipline, the perpetuation of discrimination, the continuation of the school-to-prison pipeline syndrome—if these issues are swept under the rug.

On a practical level, school officials should recognize that our courts and other relevant government agencies are becoming increasingly sophisticated in their approach to educational equity. State and federal courts are demanding the implementation of comprehensive strategies to address issues of student safety and educational equity.[16] Enforcement agencies such as the USDOE's Office for Civil Rights and the DOJ are proactively intervening in school districts based on disparate impact analysis, rather than responding only to intentional incidents of discrimination.[17]

Thus, minimizing potential legal liability requires schools to take a comprehensive approach that moves beyond piecemeal responses to specific incidents of intentional discrimination.

The solution? It's time for school leaders to apply the essential knowledge and skills reviewed in this book to engage the school community and move forward to address this challenge in a thoughtful and constructive manner. Toward that end, listed below are some common sense principles to consider, which taken together, should provide a solid basis for beginning this necessary journey in a manner that will also reduce potential legal liability.

Top Ten Tips for Moving Forward

1. Acknowledge the problem
2. Embrace the data that exists and fill the gaps
3. Have the uncomfortable discussions
4. Focus accountability on what really matters
5. Challenge your best . . . and the rest
6. Empower key stakeholders
7. Be strategic
8. Commit for the long haul
9. Celebrate success and then build on it!
10. Document, document, document

Acknowledge the problem

Acknowledging that a problem exists is a necessary first step, but is easier said than done! Much like the voter who says Congress is full of bums, but my representative is okay, there is a great temptation for school leaders to say that disparities in student discipline and related discriminatory causes may be a significant problem nationally, but not in my school or district. In fact, the mere suggestion that discrimination may be prevalent in a given school community will often illicit angry and defensive denials.

Why such a strong reaction, in light of the compelling data? Simply put, no one wants to be called a racist! We have made great strides as a nation on issues of discrimination. The vast majority of Americans pride themselves on this, and, in fact, does not engage in overt racism or discrimination. Nevertheless, this is a situation where the numbers don't lie.

Some school leaders may be willing to acknowledge that there is a problem, but argue that it is not the school district's problem, it is society's problem. According to this reasoning, the schools are simply administering their discipline policies in an impartial manner. If students of certain racial or ethnic groups are more prone to violating those policies, the argument goes, that is a larger societal challenge beyond the control of school officials. Along these lines, some school principals, staff, and parents may fear that any effort to correct the inequities in discipline outcomes will require a lowering or softening of student safety standards.

To be sure, there are certain social factors that contribute to the discipline gap. Schools cannot directly overcome issues of poverty, segregation, and social injustice, all of which may contribute to differences in student behavior and discipline. But while schools alone can't fix all of society's problems, school discipline is an issue where schools have a great deal of control through both policies and procedures, as well as the through the thoughtful, systematic implementation of the kinds of approaches and programs represented in this book.

The key to acknowledging the problem lies in not scapegoating or looking for easy answers. The discipline gap is an extremely complex issue, and there are generally a number of interrelated factors involved. The goal here should be to find common ground—all in the school community should be able to agree that providing a safe school environment is critical *and* agree that wildly varying discipline rates are a problem. The two goals are not mutually exclusive. Similar discussions have taken place for many years regarding the well-documented achievement gaps that exist between students based on race, ethnicity and, in some cases, gender. [18]

Embrace and fill the gaps

Acknowledging the problem is only the start, and will do no good if school officials fail to take the next step and begin an honest investigation of the causes of discipline gaps. This investigation should begin by reviewing the evidence that exists. But what evidence should be reviewed, and who should review it?

As to the what, there is the obvious data, such as suspension rates, expulsion rates, and the number of disciplinary infractions that have occurred, broken down by key factors such as race, ethnicity, disability, and such. Data on achievement gaps is also critical. But the analysis needs to go much deeper than these obvious measures. For example, are there large disparities in discipline referrals for certain teachers versus others? Do certain staff members tend to refer a greater percentage of minority students for discipline? If so, why do these disparities exist?

As another example, what are the perceptions of students, parents, and staff regarding your school climate and, more specifically, your school discipline policies? Are there gaps between African American and Hispanic parents and their peers in their assessment of the fairness of district discipline policies? If there are perception gaps, why do they exist?

It is important to note that data can take many forms. School officials should look for a broad range of data, that includes empirical outcome data, survey data, focus group feedback, and a wide range of anecdotal data, in order to gather a deeper understanding. This data should not be taken as a single snapshot, but should include baseline data and ongoing measures, in order to be able to assess progress over time.

As to who should gather and review data, transparency, and inclusiveness should be the guiding principles. Building trust and a sense of ownership among all stakeholders requires that school officials acknowledge the data that exists and that the development of solutions involves a broad range of stakeholders. The New Jersey Anti-Bullying Bill of Rights provides a promising model for this effort. That statute requires every New Jersey school to put in place a "School Safety/Climate Team" which is charged with reviewing school climate issues and developing school-specific recommendations. The teams include a range of school staff and parents, and can be expanded to include students. [19]

Have the uncomfortable discussions

After analyzing the data, it is likely that school leaders will need to have some rather uncomfortable discussions. For example, the school principal may need to meet with the teacher who has five times the number of disciplinary referrals as his colleagues, or the teacher who refers African American or Hispanic students at three times the rate of his colleagues. Or if survey data shows a high degree of mistrust toward the school district from parents of a certain race or ethnicity, school officials need to be willing to convene focus groups and community meetings and try to determine the underlying causes for this mistrust, and seek ways to build bridges.

While these discussions will be difficult, they can be extremely constructive, provided that all participants understand why they are occurring, how they fit into a larger effort to promote greater equity in student discipline, see that their input is taken seriously and see meaningful follow through with reasonable timelines.

Focus accountability on what really matters

It is unfortunate in today's accountability-focused educational environment, but the reality is that what gets measured gets taken seriously. [20] School officials should identify quantifiable measures that will make a real difference in promoting discipline equity and hold school staff accountable for their achievement. For example, assume that your data analysis shows that students of certain race are being disproportionately disciplined for cutting school or coming to school late. A school-wide goal could be established to reduce the number of days that students cut classes or show up late for school. Achieving this goal could involve a comprehensive effort, with ongoing communications between teachers and parents, throughout the year, and specific follow-up efforts by counselors and others when specific issues arise. Individual staff member evaluations could be in part dependent on achievement of the school-wide goal. (See the school profiles summarized in chapter 7 that illustrate some of the ways schools have successfully addressed issues like this.)

Individual accountability measures should also be implemented, based on the data. If a certain teacher has consistently larger achievement gaps than his peers, that teacher's annual evaluation should depend in part on reducing those gaps, with appropriate supports to equip the teacher to do so. If another teacher is consistently referring students for discipline for matters that should be addressed in the classroom, that too should be reflected in the teacher's evaluation, along with a requirement for appropriate, professional development. Similarly, if a certain staff member has engaged in purposeful discrimination, perhaps through the use of inappropriate language, that issue should be clearly documented in a disciplinary memo and should also be reflected in the staff member's annual evaluation.

By taking a broader approach to staff evaluation, and looking at measures that matter in closing the discipline gap, school leaders will be sending a powerful message about the importance of this issue, and will in turn gain a greater degree of buy-in from staff toward achieving the goal of discipline equity.

Challenge your best . . . and the rest

Research has consistently shown that access to experienced, highly qualified teachers is one of the most critical elements in promoting high student achievement, and that minority students and poor students tend to have lower access to such teachers.[21] Experienced, capable teachers are also effective in classroom management and engaging students, both of which contribute significantly to fewer discipline problems. Addressing this issue requires a change in school culture, so that assignment to gifted and talented, advanced placement, and other rigorous classes is no longer seen as the reward to be earned by the best or most senior staff members. Given the current lower percentages of minority students in such classes, this assignment pattern only serves to perpetuate inequities in educational opportunity.

Instead, school principals need to work with their best and most experienced teachers to gain their buy-in to the challenge to ensure that all students achieve at high levels. At the most basic level, this means a willingness to assign a school's best, most experienced teachers to classes with higher percentages of racial and ethnic minority students. Once the school's most talented teachers buy into this approach, and see it as an opportunity to be seized, it will become far easier for the school principal to gain strong buy-in from other staff members.

Empower Key Stakeholders

School leaders perpetually face the dilemma of balancing their need for strong leadership and the need to empower others. For many principals, it is difficult to let go of authority when they are then held accountable for everything that occurs in their school building. However, any experienced school principal quickly learns that he or she cannot do it all, and that empowering others is among the best strategies for ensuring continuous school improvement. [22]

This empowerment should take many forms. First, at the school district level each school district must have an individual designated to investigate claims of discrimination against students or staff members based on one or more characteristics protected under federal law. This person, often referred to as the affirmative action officer, needs to be properly trained. [23] It is unfortunately common for many school districts to appoint an affirmative action officer, hand them an outdated policy manual and tell them to go to work. If a school wishes to demonstrate that they have taken allegations of discrimination seriously, they need to be able to document that those investigating those allegations are properly trained. This should include training on how to conduct investigations, including the use of effective questioning techniques. [24]

Equally important, the school principal and district-level school officials need to assign sufficient staff and related resources to allow for thorough and timely investigations. If an affirmative action officer is overwhelmed by other allegations, or other nonrelated duties, they will inevitably take shortcuts in their investigations or have long delays in starting and completing investigations. These problems send a powerful signal to the victims of discrimination, our courts, and enforcement agencies that eradicating discrimination is simply not a priority.

Other examples of empowerment include the empowerment of school-based committees to effectively review relevant data, and develop and implement necessary recommendations for improvement. If a school safety team is created and never listened to or given the time to meet, it will quickly become apparent that the committee is not valued, and committee members will become cynical or disinterested. Our courts will also see through such efforts as window dressing intended to perpetuate the pretext that the district is taking the issue of discrimination seriously.

Be strategic

In every school community there are resources available, both internal and external, that should be part of developing and implementing a comprehensive response to discipline equity. Two overused maxims are particularly true here: school leaders should not reinvent the wheel, or act in a vacuum. Perhaps the issue of reducing adolescent crime or neighborhood violence is one that the local mayor or police chief is passionate about. Or the community happens to have very strong social service agencies in place that are open to collaborating with the schools. Or there is a small cadre of staff members who have developed a strong interest in how poor student conduct is affecting the school climate, complained about it, and might be willing to take the lead in implementing various educational reforms. There is no "one size fits all" recipe for reform. School officials need to take the time to assess their strengths and challenges.

The State of New Jersey provides an effective model for positive collaboration between education and law enforcement: the "Uniform Memorandum of Agreement Between Education and Law Enforcement."[25] This document provides a framework to guide schools and law enforcement in their interactions. It includes information on mandated collaboration areas (such as reporting incidents involving drugs and weapons) and on options for promoting greater collaboration and communication (such as information sharing regarding ongoing law enforcement operations involving students). In order to promote greater communication, school districts and local law enforcement agencies are required to annually review and adopt the memorandum of agreement.

While this process alone does not guarantee effective collaboration, it does provide detailed guidance and structure that has proven useful for many school districts in promoting positive relationships with law enforcement. For those school leaders who are resistant to this, we hear the common refrain that "I am a school leader and not a politician." But engaging the broader community and strategically moving a school district forward requires a broad set of skills, skills that are now universally recognized as being essential for effective school leaders.[26]

Commit for the long haul

As the USDOE has documented, inequities in student discipline are pervasive across the nation, and have developed and grown over a long period of time. Just as Rome wasn't built in a day, these issues cannot be resolved overnight. School officials should level-set expectations, for those involved in addressing this issue. If key stakeholders see and are part of developing a long-term plan, there is a greater likelihood that they will have a strong sense of ownership and will show patience if improvements do not occur immediately.

Many reform efforts fail because resistant staff members assume that they can outlast the reformers. But if the reform effort is not one person's crusade, and there is a strong commitment from every level of leadership—from union leadership to the school principal to superintendent to the school board and other community leaders—the message will come through loud and clear that this is not a passing fad, but an important priority that is here to stay.

Celebrate success and build on it

School leaders, by their very nature, tend to focus on the next challenge that needs to be overcome and are reluctant to declare victory until the ultimate goal is achieved. That is, in part, what makes many school leaders effective; their singular focus on achieving results. But precisely because discipline equity is a long-term challenge, it is important to celebrate successes along the way.

Perhaps a school has developed a five-year plan for overcoming significant inequities in student discipline. At the end of Year 1, the discipline gap appears nearly unchanged, in terms of out-of-school suspensions. However, the data also shows that a larger percentage of African American and Hispanic students are now taking and passing rigorous courses, or perhaps attendance rates have improved and there is some positive movement in school climate data. While the overall goal has not yet been achieved, and the progress is not across the board, we need to celebrate that some progress has been made. If we fail to recognize and celebrate these interim accomplishments, there is significant danger of burnout well before the ultimate goals are met.

Document, document, document

If it's not documented, it never occurred. While this may be a bit of an overstatement, documentation is essential—for purposes of litigation as well as for institutionalizing reform efforts. On the litigation front, there is a long history of cases where school districts have claimed that they acted responsibly in addressing issues of discrimination, but where there is little documentation to support those claims. Unfortunately, our courts are skeptical of such unsupported claims, and will often give them little or no weight in determining liability and damages.

While many school officials have become better at documentation, there is still a great deal of room for improvement. For example, when a student has been the victim of discrimination, most school officials now know to document the steps taken during the investigation process—including interviews with students, staff members, and other witnesses. But documentation of follow up efforts is often lacking. Did the school counselor meet with the victim? How often? What specific strategies and resources were provided to the parents to assist in addressing the student's needs? In terms of students who have violated school district policies, what efforts were made to work with those students and their families in order to promote positive student behaviors? What proactive steps were taken? Was a specific staff member given the role to "mentor" that student, or at least touch base proactively overtime?

For reform efforts to succeed, documentation is equally important. Are there agendas and minutes from the meetings of the school safety team? What recommendations were developed? Were they implemented? What documentation is there of the effectiveness of the reform efforts?

There is an inherent fear in this type of documentation. Once the school community has become invested in certain reform strategies, the tendency is to simply assume that they must be effective because we all believe in them. And if they are not effective, and that fact is exposed, won't it undermine the willingness to engage in future reforms?

These fears, while natural, can, and must, be overcome by school leaders. This involves setting clear expectations up front. Just as school officials must embrace the initial data documenting discipline inequities, they must embrace the data that comes in along the way on various reform efforts. Without this commitment to evidence-based reforms, school officials will repeat a common mistake of the past—simply loading one reform effort on top of another. The "initiative fatigue" that comes from this approach will inevitably undermine reform efforts and build a climate of cynicism. Conversely, by keeping reformers focused on common goals, and resisting the temptation to blindly adhere to specific reform efforts, the chances for success will increase exponentially, as will the school district's chances of properly defending against any future claims of differential treatment or disparate impact discrimination.

SUMMING UP

The U.S. Department of Education's Guiding Principles on School Discipline represent the comprehensive effort at the federal government level to document and directly address the overuse of exclusionary discipline practices. These discriminatory practices negatively affect efforts to create a prosocial school climate and come at a tremendous cost to our nation's schools.

As a legal matter these practices create significant challenges for school districts. It is critical that school leaders understand the key elements of both differential treatment and disparate impact discrimination, engage in critical self-analysis, and proactively move forward to address this issue. Not only is the right thing to do morally, socially, and economically, but it is also the single most effective strategy for reducing legal liability and protecting the legal rights of all students.

NOTES

1. This document is part of a resource package released by the U.S. Department of Education to help states, district, and schools develop local solutions that will improve school safety and discipline practices. In addition to the Guiding Principles document, the package includes the following items: (1) Dear Colleague guidance letter; (2) Directory of Federal School Climate and Discipline Resources; (3) Compendium of School Discipline Laws and Regulations; and (4) Overview of the Supportive School Discipline Initiative.

2. Tiered supports include universal, targeted, and intensive supports. Universal supports are those provided to all students before misbehavior occurs; targeted supports are those provided to students that exhibit occasional signs of mild to moderate misbehavior; and intensive supports are specific interventions that are provided to students who display frequent or severe problem behaviors, as well as to those who display risk factors.

3. To see the settlement announcement, go to http://www.ed.gov/news/press-releases/education-department-announces-resolution-civil-rights-investigation-los-angeles.

4. To see the settlement announcement, go to http://www.ed.gov/news/press-releases/education-department-announces-resolution-civil-rights-investigation-christina-s.

5. To view the entire School Discipline Guidance package, go to visit http://www.ed.gov/school-discipline.

6. See the full statement of Education Secretary Arne Duncan at http://www.ed.gov/news/speeches/rethinking-school-discipline.

7. See Attorney General Eric Holder's statement at http://www.justice.gov/opa/speech/attorney-general-eric-holder-delivers-remarks-department-justice-and-department-education.

8. For example, according to data in the Civil Rights Data Collection (CRDC) report prepared by the Office for Civil Rights in the USDOE, African American students in surveyed districts were over three-and-a-half times more likely to be suspended or expelled, as compared to their peers who are white. Research also shows that the disparities in discipline of this magnitude "are not explained by more frequent or more serious misbehavior by students of color." See page 4 of *Dear Colleague Letter* [research citations omitted].

9. The USDOE and DOJ, January 8, 2014, *Dear Colleague Letter*, points to a large body of research documenting the long-term negative consequences of disparities in student discipline, including decreased academic achievement, increased drop out problems, greater substance abuse and involvement with juvenile justice. See pages 4–5 and footnotes 8–14 of *Dear Colleague Letter*.

10. USDOE and DOJ Dear Colleague Letter (January 8, 2014), which provides the legal framework for analyzing claims of discrimination related to student discipline practices, and provides scenarios to illustrate how to apply the framework in real-world situations.

11. As the USDOE notes, a similar analysis would be used to consider claims of discrimination based on protected characteristics such as gender, disability, or religion. See page 2 and footnote 4 of *Dear Colleague Letter*.

12. See pages 10 and 13 of the *Dear Colleague Letter*, providing flowcharts to assist in analyzing each type of discrimination claim.

13. See *Dear Colleague Letter*, page 7.

14. This example is taken from the Dear Colleague letter, example 5, pages 17–18.

15. Ibid.

16. See for example the case of *L.W. v. Toms River*, 189 N.J. 381, in which the New Jersey Supreme Court outlined the affirmative obligation of school districts to act proactively to address issues of school climate, curriculum, and professional development under the New Jersey Law Against Discrimination, rather than simply responding to incidents of bullying and harassment after the fact through student discipline.

17. See for example the OCR and DOJ Settlement involving the Los Angeles School District, ordering the implementation of a comprehensive set of strategies aimed at addressing inequities in educational opportunities and discipline for limited English proficient and African American students http://www.ed.gov/news/press-releases/education-department-announces-resolution-civil-rights-investigation-los-angeles.

18. See CRDC, March 2012 Report. Addressing the achievement gap is a critical component in an overall strategy for addressing the discipline gap. Research shows that where minority students are provided greater access to rigorous academic offerings and high quality teachers, the gaps in student discipline outcomes are greatly reduced. See for example the results of Andrew Jackson School (K–8), compared to the rest of the Chicago Public Schools. One hundred percent of seventh and eighth grade African American and Hispanic students taking Algebra 1 passed, compared to 78 percent districtwide. Not surprisingly, less than 1 percent of African American and Hispanic students received suspensions, compared with 17 percent districtwide.

19. See New Jersey's Anti-Bullying Bill of Rights, P.L. 2010, c. 122.

20. Note the strong bipartisan focus on test score results under the Bush Administration's *No Child Left Behind Act* and the Obama Administration's *Race to the Top* initiative.

21. See CDRC March 2012 report, showing that schools serving the highest percentage of African American and Hispanic students are nearly twice as likely to employ first and second year teachers, and showing that overall teacher salaries are on average $2,251 less per year for teachers in those high minority schools.

22. For more information on the concept of distributed leadership, go to http://www.distributedleadership.org.

23. See USDOE *Dear Colleague Letter* (October 26, 2010) discussing school district obligations to ensure that all allegations of discrimination under federal law must be investigated in addition to any investigations required under state bullying laws. Available at http://www2.ed.gov/about/offices/list/ocr/letters/colleague-201010.pdf.

24. In New Jersey, through a partnership involving the New Jersey Department of Education, the New Jersey State Police and the Foundation for Educational Administration and its LEGAL ONE program, more than six hundred school leaders and antibullying specialists were trained during the 2012–2013 school year on how to conduct effective investigations of bullying incidents, including the use of certain questioning techniques used by law enforcement.

25. See Uniform Memorandum of Agreement Between Education and Law Enforcement at http://www.state.nj.us/education/schools/security/regs/agree.pdf.

26. See for example the Interstate School Leaders Licensure Consortium (ISLLC) Standards, which include a strong focus on community involvement.

References

Adelman, H., and Taylor, L. (2005). *The implementation guide to student learning supports in the classroom and school wide: New directions for addressing barriers to learning.* Thousand Oaks, CA: Corwin Press.

Algozzine, K., and Algozzine, B. (2007). Classroom instructional ecology and school-wide positive behavior support. *Journal of Applied School Psychology, 24,* 29–47.

Allen, J. P. and Antonishak, J. (2008). Adolescent peer influences: Beyond the dark side. In: M. J. Prinstein and K. A. Dodge (eds.). *Understanding peer influence in children and adolescents,* 141–60. New York: Guilford Press.

American Psychological Association (APA) Zero Tolerance Task Force. (2008). Are zero tolerance policies effective in the schools? An evidentiary review and recommendations. *American Psychologist* 63(9), 852–62.

Anderson, C. M., Childs, K., Kincaid, D., Horner, R. H., George, H., Todd, A. W., Sampson, N. K., and Spaulding, S. A. (2011). *Benchmarks for advanced tiers.* Eugene, OR: Educational and Community Supports, University of Oregon. Retrieved from http://www.pbis.org/blueprint/evaluation-tools.

Anderson, C. M., Lewis-Palmer, T., Todd, A. W., Horner, R. H., Sugai, G., Sampson, N. K. (2012). *Individual student system evaluation tool, Version 3.0.* Eugene, OR: Educational and Community Supports, University of Oregon. Retrieved from http://www.pbis.org/blueprint/evaluation-tools.

American Psychological Association (APA) Zero Tolerance Task Force. (2008). Are zero tolerance policies effective in schools: An evidentiary review and recommendations. *American Psychologist.* 63(9), 852–62.

Association for Psychological Science. (2008, April 16). Are humans hardwired for fairness? *Science Daily.* Retrieved December 2, 2011, from http://www.sciencedaily.com/releases/2008/04/080416140918.htm.

Atlantic Education Partners (2014, September 8). Diplomas now. In *Diplomas matter* blog. Retrieved from http://www.atlanticeducation.org/diplomas-now/.

Balfanz, R., Byrnes, V., and Fox J. (2012, December 21). *Sent home and put off-track: The antecedents, disproportionalities, and consequences of being suspended in the ninth grade.* Retrieved from http://civilrightsproject.ucla.edu/resources/projects/center-for-civil-rights-remedies/school-to-prison-folder/state-reports/sent-home-and-put-off-track-the-antecedents-disproportionalities-and-consequences-of-being-suspended-in-the-ninth-grade/balfanz-sent-home-ccrr-conf-2013.pdf.

Bambara, L. M., Nonnemacher, S., and Kern, L. (2009). Sustaining school-based individual positive behavior support. *Journal of Positive Behavior Interventions,* 11(3), 161–76.

Barrett, S., Bradshaw, C. P., and Lewis-Palmer, T. (2008). Maryland statewide PBIS initiative: Systems, evaluation, and next steps. *Journal of Positive Behavior Interventions*, 10(2), 105–14.

Barth, R. S. (2002). The culture builder. *Educational Leadership*, 59(8), 6–11.

Bass, K., Perry, S. M., Ray, A., and Berg, S. (2008). *Impact of a computer-based, social-emotional intervention on outcomes among Latino students when adult monitors of the student training are non-professionals: A randomized controlled trial.* San Francisco, CA: Rockman et al.

Bass, K., Perry, S. M., Ray, A. & Berg, S. (2008). *Impact of a self-regulated, computerized, social-emotional learning intervention on disengaged and delinquent students at a continuation high school.* San Francisco, CA: Rockman et al.

Battistich, V., Schaps, E., and Wilson, N. (2004). Effects of an elementary school intervention on students' "connectedness" to school and social adjustment during middle school. *Journal of Primary Prevention*, 24(3), 243–62.

Bear, G. G. (2010). *School discipline and self-discipline: A practical guide to promoting prosocial student behavior.* New York: The Guilford Press.

Beland, K. (2003). *Eleven principles sourcebook: How to achieve quality character education in K–12 schools.* Washington, DC: Character Education Partnership.

Benson, P. L., Scales, P. C., Hamilton, S. F., and Sesma, A. J. (2006). Positive Youth Development so far: Core hypotheses and their implications for policy and practice. *Search Institute Insights & Evidence*, 3(1), 1–12.

Berkowitz, M. (2012). *You can't teach through a rat.* Boone, NC: Character Development Group.

Berkowitz, M., Sherblom, S., Bier, M., & Battistich, V. (2006). Educating for positive youth development. In M. Killen and J. G. Smetana (eds.), *Handbook of Moral Development*, 683–702. Mahwah, NJ: Lawrence Erlbaum.

Best, J. R., and Miller, P. H. (2010). A developmental perspective on executive function. *Child Development*, 81, 1641–60.

Beyler, N., Bleeker, M., James-Burdumy, S., Fortson, J., London, R. A., Westrich, L., et al. (2013). *Findings from an experimental evaluation of Playworks: Effects on play, physical activity, and recess.* Princeton, NJ: Mathematica Policy Research, and Stanford, CA: John W. Gardner Center for Youth and Their Communities, Stanford University. Retrieved from http://www.mathematicampr.com/~/media/publications/pdfs/education/playworks_brief4.pdf.

Blum, R. (2005). *School Connectedness: Improving the Lives of Students.* Baltimore: Johns Hopkins Bloomberg School of Public Health.

Brackett, M. A., Reyes, M. R., Rivers, S. E., Elbertson, N., and Salovey, P. (2011). Classroom emotional climate, teacher affiliation, and student conduct. *Journal of Classroom Interaction*, 46, 27–36.

Bradshaw, C. P., Debnam, K. J., Koth, C., and Leaf, P. J. (2009). Preliminary validation of the Implementation Phases Inventory for assessing fidelity of school-wide positive behavior supports. *Journal of Positive Behavior Interventions*, 11, 145–160.

Bradshaw, C. P., Mitchell, M. M., and Leaf, P. J. (2010). Examining the effects of schoolwide positive behavioral interventions and supports on student outcomes: Results from a randomized controlled effectiveness trial in elementary schools. *Journal of Positive Behavior Interventions*, 12, 133–48.

Bridgeland, J. M., DiIulio, J. J., Morison, K. B. (2006). *The Silent Epidemic: Perspectives of High School Dropouts.* Washington, DC: Civic Enterprises and Peter D. Hart Research Associates.

Broderick, P.C., and Blewitt, P. (2014). *The life span: Human development for helping professionals.* New Jersey: Pearson Education.

Broderick, P. C., and Metz, S. (2009). Learning to BREATHE: A pilot trial of a mindfulness curriculum for adolescents. *Advances in School Mental Health Promotion*, 2(1), 35–46.

Brown, P. Corrigan, M., and D'Alessandro, A. (2012). *Handbook of prosocial education.* Lanham, MD: Rowman & Littlefield.

Brown, P., and Sapora-Day, B. (2008). *Professional learning communities: Building a school culture that supports learning for all.* Piscataway, NJ: Rutgers University Center for Applied Psychology.

Brown, S. National Institute for Play. (n.d.). Retrieved from http://www.nifplay.org/.

Brunn, P. (2014). Pedagogy for the Whole Child: The Developmental Studies Center's Approach to Academic, Moral, and Character Education. In L. P. Nucci, D. Narvaez, and T. Krettenauer, *The Handbook of Moral and Character Education*, 263–71. New York: Routledge.

Bry, B., Johnson, V., Chiong, A., and Urga, P. (2005). *Effects of an enhanced, peer-led group freshman prevention program on urban high school students: A pilot study.* Poster presented at the Society for Prevention Research annual conference, Baltimore.

Bryk, A. S., Bomez, L. M., Grunow, A., and LeMahieu, P. G. (2015). *Learning to improve: How America's schools can get better at getting better.* Cambridge, MA: Harvard Education Press.

Bryk, A. S., Sebring, P. B., Allensworth, E., Luppescu, S., and Easton, J. Q. (2010). *Organizing schools for improvement: Lessons from Chicago.* Chicago: University of Chicago Press.

Carter, D. S., Harris, J., and Porges, S. W. (2009). Neural and evolutionary perspectives on empathy. In J. Decety and W. J. Ickes (eds.), *Social neuroscience of empathy*, 169–82. Cambridge, MA: MIT Press.

Centers for Disease Control and Prevention. (2009). *School connectedness: Strategies for increasing protective factors among youth.* Atlanta, GA: Author. Retrieved January 30, 2012, from http://www.cdc.gov/healthyyouth/adolescenthealth/pdf/connectedness.pdf.

Character Education Partnership. (2008). *Performance values: Why they matter and what schools can do to foster their development.* Washington, DC: Author.

Cherry Hill School District. (2009). *Code of student conduct.* Retrieved from http://rucharacter.org/file/Cherry Hill High School Code of Student Conduct.pdf.

Code of Conduct. (n.d.). Retrieved September 8, 2014 from Wikipedia: http://en.wikipedia.org/wiki/Code_of_conduct.

Coffey, J. H., and Horner, R. H. (2012). The sustainability of schoolwide positive behavior interventions and supports. *Exceptional Children*, 78(4), 407–22.

Cohen, J. (2006, Summer). Social, emotional, ethical and academic education: Creating a climate for learning, participation in democracy and well-being. *Harvard Educational Review*, 76(2), 201–37.

———. (2012). School climate and culture improvement: A prosocial strategy that recognizes, educates and supports the whole child and the whole school community. In P. Brown, M. Corrigan, and A. D'Alessandro, *Handbook of prosocial education*, 227–52. Lanham, MD: Rowman & Littlefield.

Cohen, J., and Pickeral, T. (2009). *The school climate implementation road map: Promoting democratically informed school communities and the continuous process of school climate improvement* (1st ed.). New York: National School Climate Center.

Cohen, J., and Smerdon, B. (2009). Tightening the dropout tourniquet: Easing the transition from middle to high school. *Preventing School Failure*, 53, 177–83.

Collaborative for Academic, Social, and Emotional Learning. (2012).*Effective social and emotional learning programs: Preschool and elementary school edition.* Chicago, IL: Author.

Cornell, D. G. (1998). *Designing safer schools for Virginia: A guide to keeping students safe from violence.* Charlottesville: University of Virginia, Thomas Jefferson Center for Educational Design.

———. (2010). *The Virginia model for student threat assessment.* Retrieved from http://curry.virginia.edu/uploads/resourceLibrary/Virginia_Model_for_Student_Threat_Assessment_overview_paper_7-16-10.pdf.

———. (n.d.). The Virginia model for student threat assessment. Confronting Violence in Our Schools: Planning, Response, and Recovery—A PERI Symposium.

Cornell, D., Gregory, A., Huang, F., and Fan, X. (2013). Perceived prevalence of teasing and bullying predicts high school dropout rates. *Journal of Educational Psychology*, 105(1), 138–49.

Cornell, D., Sheras, P., Gregory, A., and Fan, X. (2009). A retrospective study of school safety conditions in high schools using the Virginia threat assessment guidelines versus alternative approaches. *School Psychology Quarterly*, 24(2), 119–29.

Council of State Governments Justice Center (2011). *Breaking schools' rules: A statewide study of how school discipline relates to students' success and juvenile justice involvement.* New York: Council of State Governments.

Crone, D., Hawken, L., and Bergstrom, M. (2007). A demonstration of training, implementing and using functional behavioral assessment in 10 elementary and middle school settings. Journal of Positive Behavior Interventions, 9(1), 15–29.

Damon, W. (2004). What is positive youth development? Annals of the American Academy of Political and Social Science, 591, 13–24.

Daniel, Y., and Bondy, K. (2008). Safe schools and zero tolerance: Policy, program and practice in Ontario. *Canadian Journal of Educational Administration and Policy*, 70. Retrieved from http://www.umanitoba.ca/publications/cjeap/.

Darling-Churchill, K. (2014, March 19). *Five things to know about school discipline.* Retrieved from http://www.childtrends.org/wp-content/uploads/2014/03/2014-12CT5SchoolDiscipline2.pdf.

Deal, T. E., and Peterson, K. D. (2009). *Shaping school culture: Pitfalls, paradoxes, & promises* (2nd ed.). San Francisco: Jossey-Bass.

De Long-Cotty, B. (2008). *Can computer-based training enhance adolescents' resilience? Results of a randomized control trial.* West Ed, Oakland, CA. Expanded from poster presented May 2007, at the Annual Meeting of the Society for Prevention Research, Washington, DC.

De Waal, F. B. M. (2003, November). *Morality and the social instincts: Continuity with the other primates.* The Tanner Lectures on Human Values presented at Princeton University, Princeton, NJ.

———. (2006). Joint ventures require joint payoffs: Fairness among primates. *Social Research: An International Quarterly*, 73(2), 349–64.

———. (2009). *Primates and philosophers: How morality evolved.* Princeton, NJ: Princeton University Press.

Derryberry, D., and Rothbart, M. K. (1997). Reactive and effortful processes in the organization of temperament. *Development and Psychopathology*, 55(4), 633–52.

Devaney, E., O'Brien, M. U., Resnik, H., Keister, S., and Weissberg, R. P. (2006). *Sustainable schoolwide social and emotional learning (SEL): Implementation guide and toolkit.* Chicago: Collaborative for Academic, Social, and Emotional Learning.

Dewey, J. (1916). *Democracy and education.* New York: Macmillan.

Diamond, A., and Lee, K. (2011). Interventions shown to aid executive function development in children 4 to 12 years old. *Science*, 333, 959–64.

discipline. n.d. In *Merriam-Webster.com*. Retrieved from http://www.merriam-webster.com/dictionary/discipline.

discipline. n.d. In *OxfordDictionaries.com*. Retrieved from http://www.oxforddictionaries.com/us/definition/american_english/discipline.

Durlak, J. A., Weissberg, R. P., Dymnicki, A. B., Taylor, R. D., and Schellinger, K. B. (2011). Enhancing students' social and emotional development promotes success in school: Results of a meta-analysis. *Child Development*, 82, 474–501.

Dutton-Tillery, A., Varjas, K., Meyers, J., and Smith-Collins, A. (2010). General education teacher's perceptions of behavior management and intervention strategies. *Journal of Positive Behavior Interventions,* 12(2), 86–102.

Edwards, D., Hunt, M. H., Meyers, J., Grogg, K. R., and Jarrett, O. (2005). Acceptability and student outcomes of a violence prevention curriculum. *The Journal of Primary Prevention*, 26(5), 401–18.

Eisenberg, N., and Fabes, R. A. (1992). Emotion, regulation, and the development of social competence. In M. S. Clark (ed.), *Emotion and social behavior: The review of personality and social psychology*, 119–50. Thousand Oaks, CA: SAGE Publications, Inc.

Elias, M. J. (2001). Prepare children for the tests of life, not a life of tests. *Education Week*, 21(4), 40.

Elias, M. J., Zins, J. E., Weissberg, K. S., Greenberg, M. T., Haynes, N. M., Kessler, R., et al. (1997). *Promoting social and emotional learning: Guidelines for educators.* Alexandria, VA: Association for Supervision and Curriculum Development.

Espelage, D. L., Low, S., Polanin, J. R., and Brown, E. C. (2013). The impact of a middle school program to reduce aggression, victimization, and sexual violence. *Journal of Adolescent Health,* 53 (2), 180–86.

Fabelo, T., Thompson, M. D., Plotkin, M., Carmichael, D., Marchbanks, M. P., and Booth, E. A. (2011, July). *Breaking schools' rules: A statewide study of how school discipline relates to students' success and juvenile justice involvement.* Retrieved from http://csgjusticecenter. org/wpcontent/uploads/2012/08/Breaking_Schools_Rules_Report_Final.pdf.

Fredricks, J. Blumenfeld, P., and Paris, A. (2004). School engagement: Potential of the concept, state of the evidence. *Review of Educational Research,* 74, 59–109.

Goleman, D. (2006). *Social intelligence: The new science of human relationships.* New York: Bantam Books.

Greenberg, M. T. (2006, December). Promoting resilience in children and youth: Preventive interventions and their interface with neuroscience. *Annals of the New York Academy of Sciences,* 1094, 139–50.

Gregory, A., Clawson, K., Davis, A., and Gerewitz, J. (in press). The promise of restorative practices to transform teacher student relationships and achieve equity in school discipline. *Journal of Educational and Psychological Consultation* .

Grossman, D. C., Neckerman, H. J., Koepsell, T. D., Liu, P. Y., Asher, K. N., Beland, K., et al. (1997). Effectiveness of a violence prevention curriculum among children in elementary school: A randomized controlled trial. *Journal of the American Medical Association,* 277(20), 1605–11.

Guidelines for Responding to Student Threats of Violence. (n.d.). Retrieved from http://curry. virginia.edu/research/projects/threat-assessment/guidelines-for-responding-to-student-threats-of-violence.

Hannaway, J., and Senior, A. M. (1989). *An Evaluation of the Peer Leadership Training Program: An Examination of Students' Attitudes, Behavior and Performance.* Princeton, NJ: Education Testing Service (ETS).

Highland Park School District. (2009). *Handout packet: Code of student conduct project.* Materials developed by the Center for Social and Character Development, Rutgers University under contract from the New Jersey Department of Education.

Hoffman, M. L. (2001). *Empathy and moral development: Implications for caring and justice.* Cambridge, UK: Cambridge University Press.

Holsen, I., Smith, B. H., and Frey, K. S. (2008). Outcomes of the social competence program Second Step in Norwegian elementary schools. *School Psychology International,* 29(1), 71–88.

Horner, R. H., Sugai, G., Smolkowski, K., Eber, L., Nakasato, J., Todd, A. W., and Esperanza, J. (2009). A randomized, wait-list controlled effectiveness trial assessing school-wide positive behavior support in elementary schools. *Journal of Positive Behavior Interventions,* 11(3), 133–44.

Ingram, K., Lewis-Palmer, T., and Sugai, G. (2005). Function-based intervention planning: Comparing the effectiveness of FBA indicated and contra-indicated intervention plans. *Journal of Positive Behavior Interventions,* 7, 224–36.

International Institute for Restorative Practices. (2014a). Improving school climate: Evidence form schools implementing restorative practices. Retrieved from http://www.iirp.edu/pdf/ IIRP-Improving-School-Climate.pdf.

———. (2014b). What Educators Have to Say. In Safer Saner Schools: Whole-School Change Through Restorative Practices program overview (Restorative Practices Research). Retrieved from http://www.iirp.edu/pdf/WSCOverview.pdf.

IOM (Institute of Medicine). (2013). *Educating the student body: Taking physical activity and physical education to school.* Washington, DC: The National Academies Press.

Jeannerod, M., and Anquetil, T. (2008). Putting oneself in the perspective of the other: A framework for self-other differentiation. *Social Neuroscience,* 3(4), 356–67.

Jerome, E., Hamre, B. K., and Pianta, R. C. (2009). Teacher-child relationships from kindergarten to sixth grade: Early childhood predictors of teacher-perceived conflict and closeness. *Social Development*, 18, 915–45.

Johnson, V., Holt, L., Bry, B., and Powell, S. R. (2008). Effects of an integrated prevention program on urban youth transitioning into high school. *Journal of Applied School Psychology*, 24(2), 225–46.

Johnson, V., Mun, E. Y., and Pandina, R. (2008). *A longitudinal evaluation of a peer-led transition program in a predominantly Latino high school.* Poster presented at the biennial meeting of the Society for Research on Adolescence, Chicago.

Johnson, V., Pandina, R., and Bry, B. (2008). *A peer-led prevention program delivered to a predominately Hispanic high school.* Poster presented at the Society for Prevention Research annual conference, San Francisco, CA.

Johnson, V., Pandina, R., Bry, B., Powell, S., and Barr, S. (2006). *Lessons learned from a peer-led high school transition program delivered in an inner-city school: Findings from a pilot year.* Poster presented at the Annual Meeting of the Society for Prevention Research, San Antonio, TX.

Johnson, V., Simon, V., and Mun, E. (2014). A peer-led high school transition program increases graduation rates among Latino males. *The Journal of Educational Research*, 107(3), 186–96.

Kabat-Zinn, J.(1990). *Full catastrophe living: Using the wisdom of your body and mind to face stress, pain and illness.* New York: Delacorte.

Kennelly, L., and Monrad, M. (2007). *Easing the Transition to High School: Research and Best Practices Designed to Support High School Learning.* Retrieved from http://www.betterhighschools.org/docs/NHSC_TransitionsReport.pdf.

Kincaid, D., Childs, K., Blasé, K. A., and Wallace, F. (2007). Identifying barriers and facilitators in implementing schoolwide positive behavior. *Journal of Positive Behavior Interventions*, 9(3), 174–84.

Kincaid, D., Childs, K., and George, H. (2010). *School-wide Benchmarks of Quality* (Revised). Tampa, FL: University of South Florida. Retrieved from http://www.pbis.org/blueprint/evaluation-tools.

Knafo, A., Zahn-Waxler, C., Hulle, C. V., Robinson, J. L., and Rhee, S. H. (2008). The developmental origins of a disposition toward empathy: Genetic and environmental contributions. *Emotion*, 8(6), 737–52.

Koffman, S., Ray, A., Berg, S., Covington, L., Albarran, N., Vasquez, M. (2009). Impact of comprehensive whole child intervention and prevention program among youths at risk of gang involvement and other forms of delinquency. *Children & Schools, A Journal of the National Association of Social Workers*, 31(4), 239–46.

Kohlberg, L., and Higgins, A. (1987). School democracy and social interaction. In J. Gewirtz and W. Kurtines (eds.), *Social development and social interaction*, 246–78. New York: Wiley Interscience.

Kokolis, L. L. (2007). Teaming was a catalyst for better climate and improved achievement. *Middle School Journal*, 39(1), 9–15.

Lane, K. L., Oakes, W. P., Menzies, H. M., Oyer, J., and Jenkins, A. (2013). Working within the context of three-tiered models of prevention: Using school wide data to identify high school students for targeted supports. *Journal of Applied School Psychology*, 29, 203–29.

Lassen, S. R., Steele, M. M., and Sailor, W. (2006). The relationship of school-wide positive behavior support to academic achievement in an urban middle school. *Psychology in the Schools, 43*, 701–12.

Lickona, T., and Davidson, M. (2005). *Smart & good high schools: Integrating excellence and ethics for success in school, work and beyond.* Washington, DC: Character Education.

Lohrmann, S., Forman, S., Martin, S., and Palmieri, M. (2008). Understanding school personnel's resistance to adopting SWPBS at a universal level of intervention. *Journal of Positive Behavioral Interventions*, 10, 256–69.

Lohrmann, S., Martin, S., and Patil, S. (2013). External and internal coaches' perspectives about overcoming barriers to universal interventions. *Journal of Positive Behavior Interventions*, 15(1), 24–36.

Losen, D. J., and Gillespie, J. (2012, August). *Opportunities suspended: The disparate impact of disciplinary exclusion from school*. Retrieved from http://files.eric.ed.gov/fulltext/ED534178.pdf.

Luiselli, J. K., Putnam, R. F., Handler, M. W., and Feinberg, A. B. (2005). Whole-school positive behavior support: Effects on student discipline problems and academic performance. *Educational Psychology*, 25, 183–98.

Mann, H. (1844). *Reply to the "remarks" of thirty-one Boston schoolmasters on the seventh annual report of the Secretary of the Massachusetts Board of Education*. Boston, MA: WB Fowle and N. Capen.

Marchbanks, M. P., Blake, J. J., Booth, E. A., Carmichael, D., Seibert, A. L., and Fabelo, T. (2013, April 6). *The economic effects of exclusionary discipline on grade retention and high school dropout*. Retrieved from http://civilrightsproject.ucla.edu/resources/projects/center-for-civil-rights-remedies/school-to-prison-folder/state-reports/the-economic-effects-of-exclusionary-discipline-on-grade-retention-and-high-school-dropout/marchbanks-exclusionary-discipline-ccrr-conf.pdf.

Marsh, J., and Keltner, D. (2015, April 9). How gratitude beats materialism. *DailyGood*. Retrieved from http://www.dailygood.org/story/1010/how-gratitude-beats-materialism-jason-marsh-dacher-keltner/.

Mayer, G. R. (1995). Preventing antisocial behavior in the schools. *Journal of Applied Behavior Analysis*, 28(4), 467–78.

McCraty, R., Atkinson, M., Tomasino, D., and Bradley R. T. (2009). The coherent heart: Heart–brain interactions, psychophysiological coherence, and the emergence of system-wide order. *Integral Review*, 5(2), 10–115.

McIntosh, K., Campbell, A., Carter, D., and Dickey, C. (2009). Differential effects of a tier 2 behavioral intervention based on function of problem behavior. Journal of Positive Behavior Interventions, 11, 82–93.

McIntosh, K., Doolittle, J., Vincent, C. G., Horner, R. H., and Ervin, R. A. (2009). School-wide universal behavior support sustainability index: School teams. Vancouver, Canada: University of British Columbia.

McMahon, S. D., and Washburn, J. J. (2003). Violence prevention: An evaluation of program effects with urban African American students. *The Journal of Primary Prevention*, 24(1), 43–62.

Metz, S. M., Frank, J. L. Reibel, D., Cantrell, T., Sanders, R., and Broderick, P. C. (2013) The effectiveness of the Learning to BREATHE program on adolescent emotion regulation. *Research in Human Development*, 10(3), 252–72.

Milkie, M. A., and Warner, C. H. (2011). Classroom learning environments and the mental health of first grade children. *Journal of Health and Social Behavior*, 52, 4–22.

Morgan, E., Salomon, N., Plotkin, M., and Cohen, R. (2014). *The school discipline consensus report: Strategies from the field to keep students engaged in school and out of the juvenile justice system*. Retrieved from http://csgjusticecenter.org/wp-content/uploads/2014/06/The_School_Discipline_Consensus_Report.pdf.

———. (2014). *The school discipline consensus report: Strategies from the field to keep students engaged in school and out of the juvenile justice system*. New York: The Council of State Governments Justice Center.

Murray, D. W., Rosanbalm, K., Christopoulos, C., and Hamoudi, A. (2015). *Self-regulation and toxic stress: Foundations for understanding self-regulation from an applied developmental perspective* [OPRE Report #2015-21]. Washington, DC: Office of Planning, Research and Evaluation, Administration for Children and Families, U.S. Department of Health and Human Services.

Murray, K. T., and Kochanska, G. (2002). Effortful control: Factor structure and relation to externalizing and internalizing behaviors. *Journal Abnormal Child Psychology*, 30(5): 503–14.

Muscott, H. S., Mann, E. L., and LeBrun, M. R. (2008). Positive behavioral interventions and supports in New Hampshire: Effects of large scale implementation of schoolwide positive behavior support on student discipline and academic achievement. *Journal of Positive Behavior Interventions*, 10, 190–205.

Narvaez, D. (2014). *Neurobiology and the development of human morality.* New York: W.W. Norton & Company, Inc.

National Academy of Science. (2009). *On being a scientist: A guide to responsible conduct in research* (3rd ed.). Washington, DC: National Academies Press.

National Alternative Education Association. (n.d.). *Exemplary practices 2.0: Standards of quality and program evaluation 2014.* Retrieved from http://the-naea.org/NAEA/wp-content/uploads/2014/03/NAEA-Exemplary-Practices-2.0-2014.pdf

National Middle School Association. (2003). *This we believe: Successful schools for young adolescents.* Westerville, OH: Author.

National Registry of Evidence-based Programs. (n.d.) Substance Abuse and Mental Health Administration. Retrieved from: http://www.nrepp.samhsa.gov/SearchResultsNew.aspx?s=b&q=ripple%20effects.

National School Climate Council. (2007). *The school climate challenge: Narrowing the gap between school climate research and school climate policy, practice guidelines and teacher education policy.* New York: Author. Retrieved January 29, 2012, from http://www.schoolclimate.org/climate/documents/policy/school-climate-challenge-web.pdf.

————. (2011). *National school climate standards: Benchmarks to promote effective teaching, learning and comprehensive school improvement.* Retrieved from http://www.schoolclimate.org/climate/documents/school-climate-standards-csee.pdf.

Nelson, J. R. (1996). Designing schools to meet the needs of students who exhibit disruptive behavior. *Journal of Emotional and Behavioral Disorders,* 4, 147–61.

Newcomer, L. L. and Lewis, T. J. (2004). Functional behavioral assessment: An investigation of assessment reliability and effectiveness of function-based interventions. Journal of Emotional and Behavioral Disorders, 12(3), 168–81.

New Directions Alternative Education Center. (n.d.). Retrieved from http://newdirections.schools.pwcs.edu.

NewHarbingerPub. (2013, January 25). *Learning to breathe: A mindfulness curriculum* [Video file]. Retrieved from https://www.youtube.com/watch?v=qpDBusFB9zI.

N.J.A.C 6A: 16-7. (n.d.) Retrieved from: http://www.state.nj.us/education/code/current/title6a/chap16.pdf.

Noddings, N. (2002). *Educating moral people.* New York: Teachers College Press.

————. (2008). Caring and moral education. In L. Nucci and D. Narvaez (Eds.), *Handbook of moral and character education,* 161–74. New York: Routledge.

Nucci, L. (2009). *Nice is not enough: facilitating moral development.* Upper Saddle River, NJ: Pearson Education.

Osher, D., Sandler, S., and Nelson, C. (2001). The best approach to safety is to fix schools and support children and staff. *New Directions in Youth Development, 92,* 127–154.

Osher, D., Sprague, J., Weissberg, R. P., Axelrod, J., Keenan, S., Kendziora, K., et al. (2008). A comprehensive approach to promoting social, emotional, and academic growth in contemporary schools. In A. Thomas and J. Grimes (eds.), *Best practices in school psychology,* volume 4, 1263–78. Bethesda, MD: National Association of School Psychologists.

Patterson,V., Ray, A. (2010). *Contextual sensitivity and personal trauma: Computer-based Training for SEL enables crossing domains in discipline settings.* Paper presented at 2010 Annual Conference of the American Educational Research Association. Denver, CO.

Perry, S. M., Bass, K., Ray, A., and Berg, S. (2008). *Potential and limitations of Ripple Effects self-regulated, computerized, social- emotional training to improve outcomes among students behind grade level in an unsafe and chaotic school.* San Francisco, CA: Rockman et al.

————. (2008). *Impact of a Computerized Social-Emotional Learning Intervention on African American and Latino Students When Implemented In Lieu Of Academic Instruction: A Randomized Controlled Trial.* Rockman et al. San Francisco.

————. (2008). *Impact of Ripple Effects Computer-Based, Social-Emotional Learning Intervention on School Outcomes Among Rural Early Adolescents.* Rockman et al. San Francisco.

————. (2008). *Impact of Social-Emotional Learning Software on Objective School Outcomes among Diverse Adolescents: A Summary Analysis of Six Studies.* Rockman et al. San Francisco. Expanded from poster first presented May 2007 at the Annual Meeting of the Society for Prevention Research, Washington, DC.

Project Threat Assessment. (n.d.). Retrieved from http://curry.virginia.edu/research/projects/threat-assessment.

Quinn, M. M., Osher, D., Hoffman, C. C., and Hanley, T. V. (1998). *Safe, drug-free, and effective schools for all students: What works!* Washington, DC: Center for Effective Collaboration and Practice, American Institutes for Research.

Ravitch, D. (2010). *The death and life of the great American school system: How testing and choice are undermining education.* New York: Basic Books.

Ray, A. (1999). *Impact on passivity-assertiveness-aggression of short term, computer-based, skill building in assertiveness: A pilot study.* San Francisco, CA: Ripple Effects. (White paper, first presented as peer reviewed poster session at Division of Adolescent School Health Annual conference. 1999).

———. (2008). *From multidisciplinary theory to multimedia SEL interventions: The conceptual underpinnings of Ripple Effects Whole Spectrum Intervention System.* San Francisco, CA: Ripple Effects.

———. (2008). *Unexpected findings on the impact of computerized social-emotional learning: Implications for research and practice.* Paper presented at the 2008 Annual Meeting of the American Educational Research Association. New York.

———. (2010). *Expert system theory, "the common sense—and common decency problem," and scaling social emotional learning.* Paper presented at 2010 Annual Conference of the American Educational Research Association. Denver, CO.

———. (2011). *Personalized psychosocial interventions: Children's privacy vs. schools' demand for data.* Paper presented at International Society for Technology in Education. Philadelphia, PA.

———. (2011). *The role of technology in delivering positive behavioral interventions and support.* Paper presented at International Conference on Education and New Learning Technologies. Barcelona, Spain.

———. (2011). *What computer technology can—and cannot—add to the advancement of social-emotional learning.* Paper presented at European Network for Social and Emotional Competence in Children. Manchester, England.

Ray, A., and Berg, S., (2010). *Adaptation and Fidelity with a Computerized Social-Emotional Learning Intervention Across 50 Real-World Settings.* Submitted for publication, 2010.

———. (2010). *Compliance Factors with Self-Regulated Use of A Computerized, Social Emotional Learning Intervention.* Paper presented at the Annual Meeting of American Education Research Association, Denver, CO.

———. (2010). *Factors in compliance rates with self-regulated use of Ripple Effects computer based intervention for social-emotional learning.* Paper presented at 2010 Annual Conference of the American Educational Research Association. Denver, CO.

Ray, A., Patterson, V., and Berg, S. (2008) *Impact of a district-wide individualized, computerized, positive behavioral intervention on discipline referrals, in-school suspensions and out of school suspensions.* Ripple Effects. San Francisco.

Raywid, M. A. (1994). Alternative schools: The state of the art. *Educational Leadership*, 52(1), 26–31.

Reed, B. (2008, Spring–Summer). Student engagement gains ground: A research brief. *Northwest Education*, 13(3), 37–38. Retrieved August 14, 2009, from http://educationnorthwest.org/webfm_send/434.

Rest, J. R. (ed.). (1986). *Moral development: Advances in theory and research.* New York: Praeger.

Rest, J. R., Narvaez, D., Bebeau, M. J., and Thoma, S. J. (1999). *Post conventional moral thinking: A neo-Kohlbergian approach.* Mahwah, NJ: Erlbaum.

Rimm-Kaufman, S. E., and Chiu, Y-J. (2007). Promoting social and academic competence in the classroom: An intervention study examining the contribution of the responsive classroom approach. *Psychology in the Schools*, 44(4), 397–413.

Rimm-Kaufman, S. E., Fan, X., Chiu, Y-J, and You, W. (2013). The contribution of the responsive classroom approach on children's academic achievement: Results from a three year longitudinal study. *Journal of School Psychology*, 45(4), 401–21.

Rokeach, M. (1973). *The nature of human values*. New York: Free Press.

Ross, S. W., Romer, N., and Horner, R. H. (2012). Teacher well-being and the implementation of school-wide positive behavior interventions and supports. *Journal of Positive Behavior Interventions*, 14(2), 118–28.

Ryan, W. (1972). *Blaming the victim*. New York: Vintage Books.

Sandler, S. (2000). *Turning to each other, not on each other: How school communities present racial bias in school discipline*. San Francisco: Justice Matters.

Schab, F. (1991). Schooling without learning: Thirty years of cheating in high school. *Adolescence*, 26, 839–47.

Schaps, E., Battistich, V., and Solomon, D. (2004). Community in School as Key to Student Growth: Finding from the Child Development Project. In J. E. Zins, R. P. Weissberg, M. C. Wang, and H. J. Walberg (Eds.), *Building academic success on social and emotional learning: What does the research say?* (pp. 189–205). New York: Teachers College Press.

Schick, A., and Cierpka, M. (2005). Faustlos: Evaluation of a curriculum to prevent violence in elementary schools. *Applied and Preventive Psychology*, 11(3), 157–65.

Schonert-Reichl, K. A., and O'Brien, M. U. (2012). Social and emotional learning and prosocial education: Theory, research, and programs. In P. Brown, M. Corrigan, and A. D'Alessandro, *Handbook of prosocial education*, 311–46. Lanham, MD: Rowman & Littlefield.

School District of Philadelphia. (1995). *The William Penn Foundation Report on the Implementation of the Peer Group Connection in Philadelphia High School Small Learning Communities*. Report published by the School District of Philadelphia, Philadelphia, PA.

Schore, A. N. (2003). *Affect regulation and the repair of the self*. New York: W. W. Norton & Company.

Scott, T. M., and Barrett, S. B. (2004). Using staff and student time engaged in disciplinary procedures to evaluate the impact of school-wide PBS. *Journal of Positive Behavior Interventions*, 6, 21–27.

Scott, T. M., McIntyre, J., Liaupsin, C., Nelson, C. M., Conroy, M., and Payne, L. (2005). An examination of the relation between functional behavior assessment and selected intervention strategies with school-based teams. *Journal of Positive Behavior Interventions*, 7, 205–15.

Solomon, D., Battistich, V., Watson, M., Schaps, E., and Lewis, C. (2000). A Six-District study of Educational Change: Direct and Mediated Effects of the Child Development Project. *Social Psychology of Education*, 4(1), 3–51.

Stephens, J. M., and Wangaard, D. B. (2013). Using the epidemic of academic dishonesty as an opportunity for character education: A three-year mixed methods study (with mixed results). *Peabody Journal of Education*, 88(2), 159–79.

———. (in press). The Achieving with Integrity Seminar: An integrative approach to promoting moral development in the classroom.

Sugai, G., and Horner, R. H. (2008). What we know and need to know about preventing problem behavior in schools. *Exeptionality*, 16, 67–77.

Sugai, G., Horner, R. H., Algozzine, R., Barrett, S., Lewis, T., Anderson, C., et al. (2010). *Schoolwide positive behavior support: Implementers' blueprint and self-assessment*. Eugene, OR: Educational and Community Supports, University of Oregon. Retrieved from http://pbis.org/blueprint.

Sugai, G., Horner, R. H., Lewis-Palmer, T., and Rossetto-Dickey, C. (2012). *Team Implementation Checklist, Version 3.1*. Eugene, OR: Educational and Community Supports, University of Oregon. Retrieved from http://www.pbis.org/blueprint/evaluation-tools.

Sugai, G., Lewis-Palmer, T., Todd, A., and Horner, R. H. (2005). *Schoolwide Evaluation Tool* (Revised). Eugene, OR: Educational and Community Supports, University of Oregon. Retrieved from http://www.pbis.org/blueprint/evaluation-tools.

Szalavitz, M. (2013, November 16). *Theory finds that individuals with Asperger's Syndrome don't lack empathy – in fact if anything they empathize too much*. Retrieved from https://

seventhvoice.wordpress.com/2013/11/16/new-study-finds-that-individuals-with-aspergers-syndrome-dont-lack-empathy-in-fact-if-anything-they-empathize-too-much/.

Tabibnia, G., Satpute, A. B., and Lieberman, M. D. (2008). The sunny side of fairness: Preference for fairness activates reward circuitry (and disregarding unfairness activates self-control circuitry). *Psychological Science,* 19(4), 339–47.

Threat Assessment. (n.d.). Retrieved from http://curry.virginia.edu/research/projects/threat-assessment.

U. S. Commissioner of Education (1886). *Report of the commissioner of education for the year 1884–85.* Washington, DC: U.S. Government Printing Office.

U.S. Department of Education. (2014). *Guiding Principles: A Resource Guide for Improving School Climate and Discipline.* Washington, DC: Author.

———. (2015, November 5). Statement from U.S. Secretary of Education Arne Duncan on school discipline and civil rights. *U.S. Department of Education.* Retrieved from http://www.ed.gov/news/press-releases/statement-us-secretary-education-arne-duncan-school-discipline-and-civil-rights.

Virginia Student Threat Assessment Guidelines. (n.d.). Retrieved from http://www.nrepp.samhsa.gov/ViewIntervention.aspx?id=263.

Walker, B., Cheney, D., Stage, S., and Blum, C. (2005). Schoolwide screening and positive behavior supports: Identifying and supporting students a risk for school failure. *Journal of Positive Behavior Interventions,* 7(4), 194–204.

Walker, H. M., Horner, R. H., Sugai, G., Bullis, M., Sprague, J. R., Bricker, D., and Kaufman, M. J. (1996). Integrated approaches to preventing antisocial behavior patterns among school-age children and youth. *Journal of Emotional and behavioral disorders,* 4, 194–209.

Wangaard, D. B., and Stephens, J. M. (2011). *Creating a culture of academic integrity: A tool kit or secondary schools.* Minneapolis, MN: Search Institute.

Wanless, S. B., Patton, C. S., Rimm-Kaufman, S. E., and Deutsch, N. L. (2013). Setting-level influences on implementation of the responsive classroom approach. *Prevention Science,* 14(1), 40–51.

Watson, M. (2014). Developmental Discipline and Moral Education. In L. P. Nucci, D. Narvaez, and T. Krettenauer, *The Handbook of Moral and Character Education,* 263–71. New York: Routledge.

Weissberg, M. C. Wang, and H. J. Walberg, *Building Academic Success on Social and Emotional Learning,* 189–205. New York: Teachers College Press.

Weissberg, R. P., Payton, J. W., O'Brien, M. U., and Munro, S. (2007). Social and emotional learning. In F. C. Power, R. J. Nuzzi, D. Narvaez, D. K. Lapsley, and T. C. Hunt (Eds.), *Moral education: A handbook, Vol. 2, M–Z,* 417–18. Westport, CT: Greenwood Press.

Westbrook Public Schools. (2014, March 19). School climate policy: Westbrook Connecticut (No. 5131.914). Retrieved from http://www.stamfordpublicschools.org/sites/stamfordps/files/u127/8_westbrook_11072014.pdf.

Wheelock, A., and Miao, J. (2005). The ninth-grade bottleneck: An enrollment bulge in a transition year that demands careful attention and action. *The School Administrator,* 62(3), 36.

Willis, P. (1977). *Learning to labor: How working class kids get working class jobs.* New York: Columbia University Press.

Wisconsin Department of Public Instruction. (n.d.). *Alternative education.* Retrieved from http://alternativeed.dpi.wi.gov/.

Zahn-Waxler, C., Robinson, J. L., and Emde, R. N. (1992). The development of empathy in twins. *Developmental Psychology,* 28(6), 1038–47.

Zehr, H. (2002) *The Little Book of Restorative Justice,* Intercourse, Pennsylvania: Good Books.

Zins, J., Weissberg, R. W., Wang, M. C., and Walberg, H. (Eds.). (2004). *Building school success on social emotional learning: What does the research say?* New York: Teachers College Press.

Index